German Heritage Guide

to the

Greater Cincinnati Area

Second Edition

CINCINNATI'S GERMAN HERITAGE
Cincinnati, along with Milwaukee and St. Louis, is one of the three corners of the "German Triangle," so-called for its historically high concentration of German-American residents. During the 19th century, Cincinnati was both a destination for immigrants to the tri-state area and a hub from which many groups of Germans moved inland to settle new Ohio communities — many along the Miami and Erie canal corridor which began here. German-Americans have greatly influenced the social, cultural, economic and political life of the Cincinnati area. At the turn of the 21st century, approximately half of Cincinnati's population was of German descent.

(continued on other side)

THE OHIO BICENTENNIAL COMMISSION AND THE LONGABERGER COMPANY
GERMAN-AMERICAN CITIZENS' LEAGUE OF GREATER CINCINNATI
THE OHIO HISTORICAL SOCIETY
2001   22-31

Ohio Bicentennial Historical Marker
At Sawyer Point

German Heritage Guide

to the

Greater Cincinnati Area

Second Edition

by
Don Heinrich Tolzmann

Little Miami Publishing Co.
Milford, Ohio

Little Miami Publishing Co.
P.O. Box 588
Milford, Ohio 45150-0588
http://www.littlemiamibooks.com

Cover photograph is the German Heritage Museum located at 4764 West Fork Road in West Fork
Park, Cincinnati, Ohio. Photograph is the copyright of Stevie Publishing, Inc./Robert W. Stevie.

Back cover photos and illustrations are, from top left, the Church of the Immaculata showing the
steps ascending to the church; the old North Cincinnati Turner Hall on Vine Street, Cincinnati,
from the Kevin Grace Collection in the Blegen Library at the University of Cincinnati; Johann
Roebling from the Kevin Grace Collection in the Blegen Library at the University of Cincinnati;
Ohio Historical Marker; and center, an illustration titled "View on the Rhine" as found in *Picturesque
America*, page 162.

First Edition
*   First Printing September 2003
Second Printing November 2003, corrected
Third Printing 2004, updated and corrected
ISBN 1-932250-07-7
Library of Congress Catalog Card Number 2003104567

Second Edition 2007

ISBN 978-1-932250-57-2
Library of Congress Control Number: 2007926747

Contents

Preface   *vii*

Introduction   *1*

CHAPTER 1 German Heritage Timeline   *3*

CHAPTER 2 German Heritage Highlights   *47*

CHAPTER 3 German Heritage Who's Who   *67*

CHAPTER 4 German Heritage Sites in Over-the-Rhine   *79*

CHAPTER 5 German Heritage Sites in Covington   *89*

CHAPTER 6 Museums and Libraries   *99*

CHAPTER 7 German Halls   *103*

CHAPTER 8 Local German Resources   *113*

Notes   *135*

Selective Bibliography   *139*

Index   *143*

About the Author   *155*

Tyler-Davidson Fountain

Preface to the Second Edition

Not too many works have the good fortune of going into a second edition, but the *German Heritage Guide to the Greater Cincinnati Area* proudly enjoys that honor. Since its publication in 2003, it has gone through several printings. Its purpose has been to provide an introduction to the basic dates, facts, and events relating to the history of German immigration, settlement, and influences in the region, including a guide to historic sites, libraries, and more. For this second edition a new chapter on local German resources has been added to provide useful information, especially for visitors and tourists. Moreover, information has been added throughout the *Guide*, as have a number of illustrations that were not in the first edition. Other illustrations have been enlarged, and their quality improved. Although this work serves as an introductory guide, it is one based on years of research, as well as countless hours exploring every nook and cranny in the area that might be of possible interest with regard to the German heritage. It is my hope to continually update this guide in the future, so suggestions and recommendations are always welcome. Finally, many thanks to my publisher, Barbara Keyser Gargiulo, for publishing this new edition.

Don Heinrich Tolzmann

PUBLISHER'S PREFACE TO THE SECOND EDITION

As the publisher of local and regional history in the Ohio Valley, the Little Miami Publishing Company takes great pleasure in publishing this second edition of the *German Heritage Guide to the Greater Cincinnati Area* by Don Heinrich Tolzmann. This has been one of our most popular publications, and has been well received by the general public, scholars, and students. For more than three decades, Dr. Tolzmann has been publishing works about the German heritage, and has lectured widely across the country and in Germany, earning well-deserved awards and accolades of praise. Known as well for his active community service on behalf of the German heritage, especially with regard to historic preservation, his work is greatly valued, even treasured by the community at large. We, therefore, take great pride in this new edition, and look forward to more of his valuable publications.

Barbara Keyser Gargiulo, President
Little Miami Publishing Company

INTRODUCTION

H ENRY A. FORD's *History of Cincinnati* describes the German heritage as "one of the most marked characteristics" of the area, and Henry Howe's *Historical Collections of Ohio* notes that the German element has had a great influence not only on politics and business, but also on the arts, especially in the areas of music, painting, and sculpture, and has contributed many prominent citizens to the community.[1]

Lewis A. Leonard's *Greater Cincinnati and its People: A History* observes that "the Germans of Cincinnati early became identified with the manufactures and down to the present time they have ranked among the highest engaged in fostering the great industries of the city." Leonard praises them for the contributions they have made "in brains, sinews, labor and money, toward building up Cincinnati and making it what it is today." He also finds that "the illustrious example which they have set is worthy of emulation by the coming generations, because it demonstrates the fact that the humblest, most obscure and helpless, if they cultivate industry and economy, find it possible to rise to eminence and wealth, obtain political preference, and command respect" of their fellow citizens.[2]

Leonard also notes that a history of the German element would require a lengthier work than his multivolume history of the Greater Cincinnati area, which is an accurate appraisal if all the various aspects of the German heritage were given full coverage and treatment. In the past, I have aimed to illuminate various aspects of the German heritage in a number of publications, which are listed in the Selective Bibliography, but have felt there was need for a general introductory guide.

This guide, therefore, aims to provide an introduction to the German heritage of the Greater Cincinnati area. As such, it does not aim to be a comprehensive history, but rather a survey of the general outlines of German immigration, settlement, influences, and contributions to the area. The first chapter lists some of the important dates in the history of German immigration and settlement in the region, and also aims to provide some of the flavor of the German-American experience in the time period it covers. In the second chapter some of the major aspects of the German heritage are highlighted. This is followed in chapter three by a "who's who" of some of the prominent persons of German descent, who either have been newsworthy, and/or have made significant contributions to the quality of life in the area. There are numerous historic sites of interest relating to the German heritage in the area, and in chapters four and five, I have listed some of the more noteworthy sites in the Over-the-Rhine district and Covington. And, in chapter six, I have listed the halls and clubhouses maintained by German-American societies in the region together with a brief history of each organization. A selective bibliography is provided for those interested in further reading.

Comments and suggestions are gratefully appreciated for future updated editions of this work, and may be directed to the author.

—Don Heinrich Tolzmann
University of Cincinnati

Second Printing

A few changes were made for this printing, including the correction of typographical errors.

—DHT
November 2003

Third Printing

This printing contains several corrections and additions, which aim to bring this work as up to date as possible. Many thanks to those who brought items to my attention, or made suggestions, that I have incorporated in this new printing. Finally, special thanks to the Little Miami Publishing Company for its great support in bringing out works of the author relating to the German heritage.

—DHT
January 2004

CHAPTER 1

GERMAN HERITAGE TIMELINE

T HERE ARE MANY DATES that could be identified as significant for the history of the German heritage of the region, but some of the following stand forth, while others serve as representative examples of the kinds of experiences that typified the life of German-Americans at various time periods.

The Eighteenth Century

1788–89—A few Germans are among the first settlers of the area.

1790—Major David Ziegler, a veteran of the American Revolution, arrives, along with a regiment of Pennsylvania German soldiers. They are stationed at Fort Washington, and many settle in the area, attracting others from Pennsylvania. After retiring from military life, Ziegler will settle down with his wife in Cincinnati, open a store, and then become Cincinnati's first mayor. The *Western Spy* published an obituary calling him "an honorable man to the fullest extent of the word."[1] Ziegler's wife will later move to Dayton, where Ziegler is buried at the Woodland Cemetery. The inscription at this gravesite reads:

Major David Ziegler
To whose memory this monumental
Stone is erected,
Was born in the City of Heidelberg
In the year 1748.
Having held a commission in the Army of Russia,
He migrated to Pennsylvania.
In 1774
He joined the standard of
Washington
And served with honor in the Army
Of the Revolution,
Till by the Treaty of 1783 the

Independence of his adopted country
Was acknowledged.
In the Western Country he served under
Generals Harmer and St. Clair,
And died in this city in
Sept. 1811, universally
Esteemed and respected.[2]

Fort Washington 1790

1795—Arrival of Martin Baum, businessman and industrialist, who organizes German immigration to Cincinnati by means of agents at the port cities of Baltimore, Philadelphia, and New Orleans, earning him the title of "Father" of the German immigration to Cincinnati and the Ohio Valley. According to a history of Cincinnati, "it was especially Baum (born in Hagenau, 15 July 1765; died in Cincinnati 14 December 1831), who did so much for the rise of the German element in Cincinnati and the Ohio Valley. Through his great wealth, which he had won through many different business enterprises and used again, he helped a great deal to raise the west." Baum will establish the first bank in the west, the Miami Exporting Company, and also

> called to life the first woolen factory, the first steam flouring mill, and other industrial establishments of that kind. A great number of persons found work and profit in his different factories, and since he could not find enough good and skillful workmen in the backwoods, he would enlist in Baltimore and Philadelphia newly arrived immigrants; and in this way led the first current of emigration toward the west. Moreover, the first ornamental garden, as well as the first vineyard, which Baum laid out at Deer Creek, at present within the

city boundaries, marks him as one of the most assiduous men of the west."[3]

Baum also served later as one of the early mayors of Cincinnati (after Ziegler) and was also interested in the cultural life of the area, as demonstrated by his involvement in the founding of the first public library (1802), the Western Museum (1817), and the literary society (1817). Also, he was involved with the formation of the Society for the Promotion of Agriculture (1818). His house, now the Taft Museum of Art, was open to visitors to Cincinnati, especially those involved in cultural and literary affairs.

1795–6—Christian Waldschmidt and a group of Pennsylvania Germans establish a settlement known as "Germany" on the banks of the Little Miami River. During the Civil War, the community of Germany came to be known as Camp Dennison.

1797—The first description of Cincinnati is published in Germany by Johann Heckewelder, a German Moravian missionary who had visited the area in 1792. This work attracts interest in Cincinnati, and is followed by other books written in the nineteenth century that refer to and praise Cincinnati, and lead to the formation of a positive image of the region in the German-speaking countries of Europe. Heckewelder's work has appeared in translation as *The First Description of Cincinnati and Other Ohio Settlements*. He writes of Cincinnati:

> The ground upon which the town is built is a plain along the Ohio of about two miles long; in a northerly direction it stretches say seven miles distant. The town is like as if divided into two parts, for acclivity or second bank, lies distant about 140 rods from the first bank of the Ohio. Each of these banks is about 40 feet high, and owing to their straight lines pleasing to the eye. The part below the second bank is called the lower town; but the upper town is connected with the lower. At present there are 354 surveyed lots, or city-parcels (Bürgertheile) sold and improved. To each townlot of half an acre belongs also an outlot of four acres. The conflux of people, however, is at present so great, that a lot from the second hand is readily sold at a price ranging from 30 to 60 Dollars. The town already contains 200 houses, several of which are two stones in height, well built and painted red. Houses are easily rented at from 50 to 60 Dollars per year...The population of this town is already above 900 besides the garrison and those belonging to the army, the number of which is variable. At present, however, it consists of about 200 men.[4]

The Nineteenth Century

1802—Major David Ziegler, born in Heidelberg, is elected the first mayor of Cincinnati.

Cincinnati 1802

1803—Arrival of Johannes Staebler who found employment with Martin Baum as a gardener, and planted the first vineyards in Cincinnati. Later, he is to lay out the garden of Nicholas Longworth, and is considered Cincinnati's first gardener.

1807—Cincinnati's first German publication, an almanac, *Teutscher Calender auf 1808*, appears, and indicates that already by this date there were enough Germans here to support such a publication.

1810—A Methodist missionary, Heinrich Behm, gives the first German sermons in Cincinnati.

Cincinnati 1810

1811—Martin Baum's barge, the *Cincinnati*, breaks the speed record with a trip from Cincinnati to New Orleans and back in sixty-five days.

1814—The first German congregation, the Saint Johannes–Gemeinde, is formed (today's Saint John's Unitarian Church in Clifton). In its early years, the congregation is wracked by dissension between Germans from northern and southern Germany. In 1820, meetings are to be held regarding construction of a church "and on one beautiful Sunday the Swabians and the non-Swabians became so heated about this project, that the ramshackle floor collapsed as a result of the foot-stamping and noise-making, and the squabblers were all brought together in unity in the basement below."[5]

1815—The town of Covington is laid out, and named for General Leonard Covington, whose family, originally named Korfingthan, or Kurfingthan, came from Alsace-Lorraine. Not everyone settles north of the Ohio River, and some select Covington due to its beautiful location along the river.

1819—The first German society is formed in Cincinnati, and German social life emerges, including the first beer garden.

1820s—Germans, weary of vineyard cultivation, leave Vevay, Indiana, and move to Cincinnati.

1822—The German Haydn Society performed the "Hallelujah Chorus."

1824—Cincinnati's first private German-language school opens in the German Lutheran Reformed Church. German protestant churches flourish after this date.

1825—Arrival of the first German Catholic priest in Cincinnati, Dr. Friedrich Rese, who will found the Athenaeum, from which will spring Saint Xavier College. He will write a history of the bishopric of Cincinnati, published in Vienna in 1829. German Catholic churches flourish after this date, and will become the predominant denomination of German-Americans in the region.

1825–26—Arrival of the first German artist in Cincinnati, Friedrich Eckstein, who will found the Academy of Art. Henry Howe describes him as "a man of high education and culture, man of business and affairs, [who] made art something more than a pastime, than an adjunct to the means of getting along, as his pursuits therein were governed by the high and unselfish purpose of improving the taste and refinements of his neighbors, the early pioneers of the West, and of planting the civilization of his own native Germany in his chosen American home. . . ."[6]

1826—The first German newspaper appears, *Die Ohio Chronik*. Altogether, almost two hundred newspapers and journals will be published in the German language in Cincinnati, and will provide a wealth of historical data, especially biographical information.

1827—Karl Anton Postl, a well-known German-American author (pseudonym: Charles Sealsfield) writes of Cincinnati in his well-known book *Die Vereinigten Staaten von Nordamerika*: "There is no doubt that the commanding situation of this beautiful town, its majestic river, its mild climate, which may be compared to the south of France, and the liberal spirit of its inhabitants, contribute to render this place, both in physical and moral points of view, one of the most eligible residences in the Union."[7]

1829—In the most influential book in the history of the German immigration, *Bericht ueber eine Reise nach den westlichen Staaten Nordamerikas*,[8] Gottfried Duden writes: "Cincinnati is called the most beautiful city of the entire West, and truly the European who involuntarily associates all kinds of ideas about savage life with the words American interior, would scarcely trust his eyes if he could suddenly be transported from his home to this city."

1830s—This decade begins the massive waves of German immigration to America due to discontent with the political, economic, and social conditions in Europe. Many come to the region, especially from northern Germany.[9]

1831—The Miami-Erie Canal is completed, which later becomes known as the Rhine and the district it embraced as the Over-the-Rhine district, where Germans congregated in the nineteenth century. It was said that when you crossed over the bridges going into the district that you were going "over the Rhine." One commentator described the district as follows:

Over-the-Rhine

Cincinnati's German community, in its early years, was concentrated largely in the area north of where the canal entered the city, and was known as "Over-the-Rhine." Here the Germans lived in neat little frame and brick houses built flush with the sidewalk, and with backyards fenced in with lattice work and planted with flower and vegetable gardens. Every Saturday, German housewives scrubbed the front steps of their homes until they were snow white. Here too the German Hausfrau nourished her family with German food and delicacies which quickly became part of the American culinary art. After working hours and on Sunday, the men sought recreation in the taverns, played euchre, skat and pinochle, or brought their families to the beer gardens to listen to old familiar German airs.[10]

Michael Werk, born at Marlenheim in Alsace, arrives in Cincinnati, where he establishes the M. Werk & Co., which specializes in candle and soap-making—by-products of the growing meat-packing industry. His Werk's Tag Soap is most likely the first bar soap produced in the United States.

1834—The German Society is formed as a mutual aid society for the recently-arrived German immigrants.

A Beer Garden on the Rhine

1836—The *Volksblatt*, the first German daily newspaper in Cincinnati, begins publication, and is edited by Heinrich Roedter, who fled his homeland in the Palatinate as a result of his involvement in the political protest demonstration known as the Hambacher Fest. He makes the *Volksblatt* the most influential German-American newspaper in the Ohio Valley.

Also, in 1836, the first decorated Christmas tree in Cincinnati was set up by Ludwig Rehfuss, a druggist who was active in German-American community affairs.

1837—Christian Burkhalter, former secretary to Prince Bluecher, establishes a newspaper, the *Westlicher Merkur*. Also, appearing that

... Das ...

Cincinnatier Volksblatt

(Gegründet 1836)

ist die älteste und hervor=
ragendste deutsche Zeitung
im mittleren Westen. = = =

Geschäftsstelle:

127 Ost Siebente Straße,

zwischen Walnut und Main Str.

year is the first German Catholic newspaper in the United States, *Der Wahrheitsfreund*, edited by Johann Martin Henni. The German Lutherans begin their own newspaper, *Der Protestant*. In the following year, the German Methodist newspaper, *Der Christliche Apologete*, commences publication and continues to 1941.

1838—Further dissension at the Saint Johannes–Gemeinde causes members from Osnabrueck and the surrounding area to withdraw, and establish the North German Church, on the west side of Walnut Street, between Eighth and Ninth streets. According to Emil Klauprecht: "In order to avoid any future difficulties, the new congregation included in their constitution the requirement that every trustee had to be able to speak Low German."[11] The dissension in the church is due to regional and dialectal differences between Germans from northern and southern Germany, with the former stressing the use of Low German, and the latter the use of High German.

German immigrants lose their lives in the harbor of Cincinnati as a result of an explosion on the steamer, *Moselle*. According to Klauprecht, "While the steamer was docked . . . the captain, with criminal negligence, had held back the steam, which the fire had built up in the meantime, in order to demonstrate the vessel's speed while passing the entire length of the city, and also to catch another boat ahead of him, which had just shortly before departed to Louisville . . . the boilers blew up with a thunderous roar. With that there was a horrible loss of human life. Bodies and parts of bodies flew into the air accompanied by screams of the horribly injured. . . . Fifteen minutes after the explosion the boat sank. It had been packed full with between-deck passengers, including 250 German immigrants, most of whom drowned in the river. . . . Countless parts of bodies were scattered all along the river bank."[12] The news of the accident alone indicates how many German immigrants are coming down the Ohio River on a regular basis.

1840—The first German-language public school opens in the Third German Protestant Memorial Church, and others will soon follow.

Also, German Jews establish a congregation, B'nai Yeshrum, which reflects the increased German Jewish immigration.

City Council begins printing ordinances in German, demonstrating the growing influence of the German element, which now numbered fourteen thousand out of a total population of forty-five thousand.

1842—First major nativist riot takes place, and is referred to as the *Hermannsschlacht*, or the Battle of Hermann. Bricks are thrown, shots are fired, and a constable is severely wounded. German-Americans hold mass meeting, and pass resolutions against the nativism and the anti-immigrant Know-Nothing movement.[13]

Maifest is celebrated in Cincinnati, which is promoted by Heinrich Roedter, editor of the *Volksblatt*. The May festival not only celebrates the advent of spring, but it also has a political connotation, as it honors the tenth anniversary of the Hambacher Fest, a political protest in Germany, which took place in May 1832.

Former President Martin Van Buren comes to Cincinnati on his trip west, and is met by a delegation of German vintners, who presented him with a variety of wines they had produced from grapes grown during Van Buren's administration.

1843—The first German plays are presented, and several German theaters will come into being thereafter, and will flourish into the twentieth century.

A Catholic church is dedicated in Covington with Father Ferdinand Kuehr as its pastor, who is considered the Catholic patriarch of Covington. In 1870/71, the church is replaced by the Mother of God Church.

1844—A German Reading and Cultural Society is organized, reflecting the growing interest in German-language reading materials.

1846—During the Mexican War voluntary Cincinnati German units are formed. According to Klauprecht, "the German units of the American troops demonstrated particular bravery in this campaign."[14]

1848—The failure of the 1848 Revolution in the German states cause many Forty-eighters to immigrate, followed by large waves of immigration. They form the oldest German society in Cincinnati, the Cincinnati Central Turners, the first Turner society in America, and they construct Turner Hall in Over-the-Rhine, which is to be dedicated in 1850. The Turners' philosophy is best summed up in their motto, "A Sound Mind in a Sound Body," as they believe in keeping physically and intellectually fit.

1849—The German Orphan Home is founded as the German General Protestant Orphan Home after a cholera epidemic leaves countless children homeless. It is the result of the united effort of German Protestant churches in the area. In 1950, the name will change to

German Orphan Home, Cincinnati, Ohio.

German Orphan Home

Beech Acres. Residential care will end by the 1980s and Beech Acres will focus on parental care issues in accord with its mission of "strengthening families for children."

1850s—Cincinnati is not only a destination for German immigrations, but a distribution center for immigrants throughout the region. Also, colonization and settlement societies are formed in Cincinnati that establish daughter settlements across the country, including settlements at Teutopolis, Illinois; Guttenberg, Iowa; New Ulm, Minnesota; Buffalo, Wisconsin; Tell City, Indiana; Wartburg, Tennessee; and Windhorst, Kansas. (See, for example, the cannon at the Brown County Historical Society Museum in New Ulm, Minnesota, which was presented to the town by the Cincinnati Turnverein to protect itself after the 1862 Sioux Uprising there.)

Carl Wittke describes the image of German-Americans at mid-century: "By the middle of the nineteenth century, the everyday life of the Germans of Cincinnati had produced a certain German stereotype in the minds of many native Americans. They were usually represented with heavy beards and mustaches and wearing soft hats in contrast with the smooth-shaven faces and high stiff hats of the Americans. They were respected for their thrift, and for their competence. . . . Mingled with this picture of the competent, industrious and successful German craftsman and storekeeper was that of the German who loved his beer garden, his long pipe, and the music of his German bands, orchestra, and singing societies."[15] And, most of them "vigorously combated what they called the 'Puritan Sabbath,' as they feel that Sunday afternoon should be a time for family get-togethers, picnics, and festivity."

In 1850 Cincinnati has thirteen breweries and by 1860 will have thirty-six, which clearly reflects the tastes of the increasing German population of the region.

1852—By this time, Cincinnati Germans have formed five militia companies, which create a regiment consisting of 230 members. These units were organized originally for defense against the Know-Nothings, but eventually they will become part of the state militia, subject to call by the governor.

1853—The Bedini Riot takes place as Cincinnati Germans protest the arrival of the Papal Nuncio Bedini in December, as he had opposed the 1848 Revolution in Italy. What starts out as a demonstration quickly turns into a riot. Klauprecht notes:

> Evidently the police sought to handle the demonstration as a dangerous riot. Rather than read the riot act, which would have called on the people to disperse, (the police captain) gave the command to arrest all the demonstrators. The police carried out the order in a brutal manner. At the outset of the first attack a shot was fired, no one knows by which party, to be followed in an instant by several dozen more. Then those in the procession, some armed with swords and pistols, and who outnumbered the police ten to one, broke and scattered wildly, accompanied by the screams of women and children. The police, seized by their sudden victory, fell upon those fleeing and arrested them in droves, striking and hitting them with a savage fury, while dragging them to the police station.[16]

Later, all charges relating to the incident are dropped, but they clearly reflect the Zeitgeist.

1854—German-American organizations from Cincinnati and across Ohio meet and endorse the Louisville Platform, which is a position statement formulated by Forty-eighters in Louisville, and which is adopted at similar meetings elsewhere in the country. It provides insight into where German-Americans stand on the issues of the day, and is widely distributed in German and English. It is addressed to

"All true Republicans in the Union," and proclaims that its goals are "Liberty, prosperity and education for all." Cincinnati German historian Emil Klauprecht describes the platform as a declaration of war against all forms of oppression and slavery. Indeed, it calls slavery "a political and moral cancer," and advocates its elimination. It also supports a wide range of positions, and supports democracy by direct election, as well as women's rights. Not surprisingly, it strongly supports personal liberty, which it defines as opposition to "the interference of law into the sphere of the individual." And, in specific, it condemns temperance laws not only as unconstitutional, but as "tyrannical encroachments upon individual liberty and narrow-minded manifestations of an entire misconception of the legislative duties."[17] The platform reflects how German-Americans derive a political philosophy based on principle, and that one of the most important of them was their concept of "personal liberty."

1855—Anti-immigrant–Know-Nothing riot takes place. In 1856, another Know-Nothing riot will take place in Covington, and members of the Turners are attacked. The outburst of nativism tends to draw German-Americans more closely together on both sides of the river.[18]

1856—Friedrich Gerstaecker, a German-American author, writes, "Cincinnati, the Queen of the West, the El Dorado of the German emigrant! Ask a German, who is traveling into the interior from one of the seaports, Where are you going? and the answer will invariably be—to Cincinnati!"[19]

1859—The Schiller celebration marks the centennial of the birth of the German poet Friedrich Schiller.

The "Church of the Steps," or Immaculata, is constructed from stone from the slopes of Mount Adams. A historical marker at the church will read "Early it was known as the 'Archbishop's Church' in honor of Archbishop John Purcell (1800–83) who

"Church of the Steps"
or Immaculata

donated the land and supervised construction. It was conceived as a votive offering for his safety at sea during one of his many journeys to Europe. Since 1860 it has been the site of the annual Good Friday Pilgrimage where the devout say prayers on each step to the summit. Originally the parish served the German-speaking Catholics of Mount Adams. In 1970 it was consolidated with the nearby Holy Cross Parish and is now known as Holy Cross–Immaculata Church. The interior murals were painted by Johann Schmitt, teacher of American artist Frank Duveneck." It should be noted that the murals with German-language inscriptions are some of the most beautiful in a church in the region.

Mural by Johann Schmitt inside Church of the Immaculata.

1860—Thirty percent of a population of 161,044 in Cincinnati is of German stock.

1861—President Abraham Lincoln is greeted on his way to Washington, D.C., by a Cincinnati German delegation, and a message is read to him, most likely written by August von Willich, that praised Lincoln for his recent election victory, and promised him continued support: "We firmly adhere to the principles, which directed our votes in your favor. We trust, that you the self-reliant because self-made man, will uphold the Constitution and the laws against secret treachery and avowed treason. If to this end you should be in need of men, the German free workingmen, with others, will rise as one man at your Call, ready to risk their lives in the effort to maintain the victory already won by freedom over Slavery."[20] Note that in the election, Lincoln will carry Cincinnati by twenty-two hundred votes and Hamilton County by only eleven hundred votes, so that the German vote will become crucial to his victory here.

As the Civil War breaks out, Judge John B. Stallo speaks at a mass meeting, stating that since immigrants have the same rights as the native-born, they too must fight for and protect the Union.[21] Cincinnati Germans enthusiastically support the Union cause, forming four of the seven regiments from Cincinnati in the Civil War, including the Ninth Ohio Regiment formed by the Turners.

1862—The Covington Altar Build Stock Company, also known as the Institute of Catholic Art, begins to design and decorate German Catholic churches throughout the Ohio Valley with works of art produced by German-American artists.

1865—Henry Wielert opens what will become one of the favorite saloons in the Over-the-Rhine district, Wielert's, which is located on Vine Street. This is a large beer hall that will become known for serving Hauck's beer, and provides an Old World ambience accompanied by German music. Among the many other popular saloons and beer gardens were the Lower Garden, the Atlantic Garden, the Pacific Garden, Schickling's, Schuler's, Schumann's, etc. Saloons and beer gardens

Wielert's Beer Hall

are popular not only because of the brew they serve, but also because they maintain the free lunch tradition, designed to whet your thirst and draw in customers. On the free lunch menu are items such as wurst, ham, roast beef, herring, sardines, cheese, crackers, breads of all kinds, Kartoffelsalat, pickles, radishes, etc.

1866—Civil War veterans form the Cincinnati Schuetzen-Verein and sponsor the Schuetzenfest, Cincinnati's oldest German-style festival.

1867—The Suspension Bridge is completed by Johann August Roebling, and serves as the model for the Brooklyn Bridge.

Roebling Suspension Bridge

1869—The German Pioneer Society of Cincinnati is formed, and publishes a historical journal, *Der Deutsche Pionier.* Branches of the society are also formed in Covington and Newport. By 1877, the society will have nearly a thousand members. At monthly meetings, members relate their life stories as German pioneers, and later the meetings will feature lectures on literature, educational issues, German culture, travelogues, and humorous presentations. The society will continue until 1961, when it will have only sixty members remaining.

A monument, now located in Memorial Hall in Over-the-Rhine, is dedicated, which lists the Civil War casualties from the Ninth Ohio Regiment.4

1870—The area demonstrates great enthusiasm and support for German unification by Otto von Bismarck by means of the Franco-Prussian War. August von Willich, who had organized the Ninth Ohio and Thirty-second Indiana Regiments during the Civil War, travels to Berlin and offers his services, but due to age, his offer is not accepted.

1871—Tyler Davidson Fountain from Munich, Germany, is dedicated, and the German fountain becomes a symbol of the city. Cincinnati's first citywide May Festival is also held and will become the oldest choral festival in the United States. Also, the Board of Education creates the German-English Normal School dedicated to the training of teachers for the public schools.

1872—Grammer's Restaurant opens on Walnut Street in Over-the-Rhine, and will become the oldest pre-Prohibition German restaurant to remain in the old German district, ultimately to remain open only to private parties.

Tyler-Davidson Fountain

1873—Cincinnati Zoo is built due to the efforts of Andreas (Andrew) Erkenbrecher, and the first citywide May Festival is held.

The German-American Free Kindergarten Association is formed for the purpose of sponsoring a German-bilingual kindergarten based on the educational principles of Friedrich Froebel. Suitable rooms for the kindergarten, which opens in November 1873, are found near the Saenger-Halle, by Washington Park, as the park is considered an excellent playground for children. A teacher is engaged who had just arrived from Germany, bringing a letter of recommendation from the Duchess of Coburg, under whose patronage she had conducted a kindergarten. The Association sponsors musical programs, such as the Children's May Festival, held at the Music Hall, and by the end of the century has more than six hundred pupils at seven schools in Cincinnati. According to an 1897 Children's May Festival program, the Association was German-American because the program was bilingual, but pupils "are, and know themselves to be Americans, and differ from their compatriots only in enjoying the privilege of learning, without effort, two languages instead of one—an advantage readily perceived by every progressive mind."[22]

1874—H. A. Rattermann begins editing the historical journal, *Der Deutsche Pionier*, published by the German Pioneer Society of Cincinnati, which commenced publication in 1869, and becomes the major nineteenth-century German-American historical journal. In an address before the Covington branch of the Society, Rattermann states that the society is working hard "to raise the spirit of self among its members and to make known the history and the cultural development of the Germans in this country."[23]

1875—Music Hall is built with donations ($125 thousand) from Reuben Springer, a Kentucky German. In the statewide campaign for governor, German-Americans mobilize in support of Rutherford B. Hayes, who runs for his third term. Carl Schurz speaks at Turner Hall on behalf of Hayes.

1878—Hubert Heuck, owner of Heuck's Opera House, opened his theater on Sundays, which is considered in violation of an Ohio law against "performing common labor on a Sunday." The *Cincinnati Enquirer* (6 May) reports that the raid of Heuck's place "excited considerable comment throughout the city" and "the general feeling seemed to be against the action, which was

Springer Music Hall

considered Puritanical and Quixotic, to say hairsplitting in its discrimination." All charges in the matter are dropped, except against Heuck, as the "State introduced witnesses to prove that beer was sold on the premises, but in a trial by jury he was found not guilty."

1880s—German-Americans bolster the economic and industrial foundations of the city in brewing, banking and finance, baking, meatpacking, and the machine industry.

1880—In Cincinnati, there are 1,837 saloons serving a population of 225,000, or one for every 122 inhabitants.

1881—Arrival of Hermann von Wahlde in Cincinnati as a German teacher in the public schools. He publishes a poetry volume, *Natur und Heimath*, which covers many topics and themes relating to the German-American experience, and is representative of the many German-American authors in the region, most of whom belonged to the German Literary Club.

Brewer John Hauck purchased the park for the Cincinnati Zoo for $135 thousand and leased it to the zoo for ninety-nine years, and thereby saved the zoo for the city. This is but one example of the philanthropy practiced by German-Americans in the brewing and business community.

Headwaiter, Louis Mecklenburg, purchases John Neeb's Mount Auburn Garden Restaurant and Billiard Saloon, begun in 1865, and begins Mecklenburg Biergarten in Corryville, east of the University of Cincinnati, and will later become the only surviving pre-Prohibition beer garden in the area.

1882—Andrew Jergens, who came from Germany with his parents, founds the Andrews Soap Company, which became Andrew Jergens and Company.

1883—The bicentennial of the founding of the first German settlement in America at Germantown, Pennsylvania, is celebrated on 6 October. Thereafter, the October date comes to be known as "German Day," and attempts are made to celebrate it on an annual basis.

Heuck's new Opera House opens, and is considered one of the most beautiful theaters in Cincinnati. Max Burgheim describes the opening as "a true event for Cincinnati, which long had felt sensitive about the lack of an elegant opera house," and soon those who do not want to go "over-the-Rhine" come to Heuck's on a regular basis. This is made possible "through the untiring efforts of Mr. Heuck, to offer his audiences the best. . . . As a result, Mr. Heuck, for his energetic efforts has found the fair reward and enjoys today not only a universally esteemed name, but also can with tranquility see the future in his eyes (look into the future)."[24]

1886—John Robertson published *The Last Strike for Liberty: A Semi-Political Satire on the Revolutionary Demands of the Liberal Foreign Element*,

German Deaconess Home and Hospital

which espoused nativist antipathies reminiscent of the 1850s Know-Nothing era. Robertson identifies the foreign element in his preface as "the so-called 'liberal' German element," and claims that it "would abrogate the Sabbath, displace churches with Sunday theaters, beer gardens and concert halls, and maintain a saloon on every corner of the street," and that it, moreover, was "not the stuff of which great and prosperous nations are made." He also asserted that "the nation honors those vigorous, industrious Germans," but that those who find "the laws of the United States . . . too puritanical to suit their ideas, they must return to the effete despotisms from whence they came." No doubt, Robertson was referring to German-American opposition to the prohibition movement, and especially to Sunday "blue laws," which they felt were Puritanical infringements on their "personal liberty."[25]

1888—*Das Diakonissen Krankenhaus*, the Deaconess Hospital, was founded in 1888 by Sisters Kypke and Sophie Munde from Germany, who were deaconesses, or Protestant church women, dedicated to helping the sick and needy. They opened their hospital in the Over-the-Rhine district at 533 East Liberty Street. They had been invited here by the *Evangelisch Protestantischer Verein fuer Diakonie*, or Evangelical Protestant Society for Deaconess Work and Care for the Sick, a group of more than a dozen congregations that had gotten together to organize and sponsor a hospital and a motherhouse for deaconesses. Such orders flourished in Germany, and came to America by means of the German immigration. Deaconess Hospital today is located on Straight Street near Clifton Avenue and is another part of the legacy of the German heritage of the area.

1889—The Twenty-fifth National Turnfest is held in Cincinnati with 1,517 participants representing ninety-three Turner societies. For many years, this fest is considered the model Turnfest.

The Superintendent of the Cincinnati Public Schools, John B. Peaslee, states in an address: "I not only thoroughly believe in the German department of our public schools, but I am convinced that it would be better for the intellectual development of our pupils if they all studied the German language in connection with the English."[26]

1890—Fifty-eight percent of Cincinnati's population of 297,000 is of German stock.

The Altenheim (German Old Men's Home), Cincinnati, Ohio.

The Altenheim

1891—The *Altenheim* was organized in 1891 as a home for elderly German men by members of the German-American elite, and included the following families as sponsors: Alms, Schmidlapp, Moerlein, Wielert, Muehlaeser, Erkenbrecher, Markbreit, and Tafel. In the *Altenheim's* garden an oak tree from Germany was planted in honor of Otto von Bismarck. As a result of World War I, the *Altenheim* changed its name to the Cincinnati Old Men's Home, and then later changed to the Home for Aged Men. The Altenheim building was demolished after the grounds were acquired in 1966 by the Children's hospital. Nevertheless, it represents the kinds of institutions founded by the philanthropic members of the German-American community.

1893—In Cincinnati, the average per capita consumption of beer is forty-one gallons, compared to the national average of sixteen gallons—just one more indication of the German flavor of the area.

1895—Cincinnati's first annual German Day is held at the zoo and leads to the formation of the German Day Society, the umbrella organization for the area's German-American societies, which will later become the German-American Alliance. The first German Day is a result of the celebration of the German-American bicentennial in 1883, and the attempts, thereafter, to place this on a regular annual schedule. German Day continues to be celebrated until World War I (1916), and then again in the 1920s and 1930s, and then again after the Second World War.

1896—Rev. A. H. Walburg, pastor of Saint Augustine's Church, publishes a book, *German Language and Literature*, that explains the significance of German culture and what it means to be German-American. He writes about those who grew up German-American, stating "My lot was cast in such fortunate circumstances. My cradle stood not, on the banks of the Rhine nor on the Elbe, but on the banks of the beautiful Ohio. Yet I am German to the core as though I were born in Germany." He explained:

> I am both German and English, or a German-American and an English-American. I read Shakespeare and Milton with all the pleasure and appreciation of an Englishman; I pick up Goethe and Schiller and understand and enjoy as fully as any German. I meet English-speaking people and am one of them in thought, in sentiment, in habits, in language. I turn to a German company and am instantly transformed into a German assimilating with them and entertaining thoroughly into their spirit, their life, their sympathies. This priceless possession of two mother tongues, of two lives, this dual existence, is something so delightful, charming, and precious, as to be indescribable. Here then the impossible is made possible. It was always held that a person could have but one mother tongue. The German-American however can have two, and one as fully, as thoroughly, as completely as the other. . . . The possession of these two languages is of priceless value. It broadens the views, opens new fields of knowledge and research. . . . [27]

1898—A directory lists twenty-six breweries in Cincinnati and Covington, including the Bavarian Brewing Company, the John C. Bruckmann Brewery, the Germania Brewing Company, the John Hauck Brewing Company, the Christian Moerlein Brewing Company, the George Wiedemann Brewing Company, and The Windisch-Muehlhauser Brewing Company.

1899—National Saengerfest is held in Cincinnati, and is sponsored by North American Saengerbund, the federation of German-American singing societies.

The Twentieth Century

1900s—The expanding German-American population moves southward to northern Kentucky and to the west side of Cincinnati. This leads to an east side/west side dimension to the region, which is based on the concentration of those of German descent on the west side and in northern Kentucky.

1900—Establishment of the German Department at the University of Cincinnati.

1902—German-American societies are actively engaged in civic affairs

Cincinnati Maennerchor (Cincinnati German Men's Choir)

on a wide variety of issues, as readily exemplified by an article published in the *Cincinnati Commercial Tribune* (24 March 1902) titled "German Societies Want Low Street Car Steps." The article reports:

> The local German societies are to take up the fight for low steps on summer street cars and it will be prosecuted by them in earnest.
>
> The Hessischer Unterstuetzungsverein (Hessian Benevolent Society) yesterday took the initiative and passed resolutions which will be placed before the Board of Legislation. The resolutions cite that low steps are universally desired by the patrons of the company, as the present ones are unreasonably high, and that most times dangerous for ladies, elderly or fleshy men or women to use.
>
> There is now being tried on a car at the Chester Park shops a new adjustable step, which the committee from the society has viewed with favor, and it desires that either that arrangement be adopted or some other as good.
>
> The Board of Legislation is asked to take the proper steps such as may be necessary to bring about its adoption by the street car company for some practical and adjustable step.
>
> Other German societies will adopt similar resolutions at their next meeting.

1904—Henry Moeller becomes the first German-American archbishop of Cincinnati.

1906—Judge John Schwaab is elected president of the German-American Alliance, the umbrella organization of area German-American societies, and serves until 1919. He also serves as president of the Ohio German-American Alliance, and as a vice president of the National German-American Alliance.

1909—The National German-American Alliance holds its national convention in Cincinnati, which reflects the leadership role played by Cincinnati in German-American affairs. The convention fills the Music Hall, where the meetings are held. The Cincinnati chapter of the Alliance serves as host of the convention, which attracts delegates from forty-two states. Judge John Schwaab, president of the Cincinnati chapter, also serves as president of the state chapter, the Ohio German-American Alliance, and as a vice-president of the National

Postcards depicting the National Turnfest in Cincinnati, Ohio, in June 1909. Printed with permission from the collection of Don Prout, Web site <www.cincinnativiews.net>

Alliance. According to the *New York Times*, Dr. Charles Hexamer, national president, responds to the greetings of Mayor John Galvin, with an address that 'emphasizes the opposition of German-Americans to Prohibition:

> As devoted citizens of this country, we hold ourselves second to none in our devotion to the cause of true temperance and to all that makes for the sanctity of home and decency and order in the State, but we are bitterly opposed to the passage of any law that destroys our rights of personal liberty.

As devoted citizens of this country, we hold ourselves second to none in our devotion to the cause of true temperance and to all that makes for the sanctity of home and decency and order in the State, but we are bitterly opposed to the passage of any law that destroys our rights of personal liberty.

As free and sovereign people we believe we have the right to regulate our lives as we see fit. The right to drink our wine and our beer, we consider as absolute as an attribute of human liberty as is the right to buy any other food.

The divine right of each to pursue his own good in his own way should not be sacrificed to the fears and fanaticism of those who regard or pretend to regard drink as a crime.

Hexamer states: "We German-Americans have never allowed our love of food or drink to degenerate into intemperance or to interfere with the good of the community," and that Prohibition is "an unrighteous invasion" of human rights and human freedom. He closes with the hope that "the spirit of liberty and American fair play" will triumph over those that favor Prohibition.

The Schiller Celebration culminates in the performance of *Wilhelm Tell* at the Music Hall.

1910—The two major German newspapers in Cincinnati, the *Volksblatt* and the *Freie Presse*, have a combined aggregate circulation of ninety-two thousand.

President William H. Taft attends the May Festival with the German Ambassador, Count Johann Heinrich von Bernstorff, and is welcomed by a large crowd, including five hundred school children. After the intermission, President Taft dedicates the statue of the festival's first musical director, Theodore Thomas, which will remain located in the foyer of Music Hall. At an evening dinner at the Queen City Club three toasts are presented: to the President and Mrs. Taft; to Germany and the German Ambassador; and to the May Festival.

1914—The German-Austro-Hungarian Aid Society of Cincinnati is formed by Cincinnati Germans to aid those in need, such as widows and orphans, in Germany and Austro-Hungary, as a result of the war. By the time of the United States involvement in the war, in 1917, nearly $80,000 will be raised through a variety of fund-raising events such as festivals, programs, and lectures.

Souvenir card of the German-Austro-Hungarian Aid Society of
Cincinnati. Printed from the collection and with the permission of
Don Prout, Web site <www.cincinnativiews.net>

1915—The German bilingual program in the Cincinnati Public
Schools consists of 175 teachers and 17,000 students.

1917–18—World War I results in anti-German hysteria and sentiment.
An Ohio Historical Society marker, entitled "Anti-German Hysteria,"
originally was located in Clifton Heights and is now scheduled for
removal to Findlay Market. It reads as follows:

> The United States' declaration of war on Germany in April 1917
> resulted in a tragic display of hysteria directed against everything and
> anything German. In Cincinnati, German teachers were dismissed
> from public schools, German professors were censored, German
> collections and publications were removed from circulation at the
> Public Library, businesses with German names had their names
> "Americanized," and by police order, only English language public
> meetings could be held. As a result of the anti-German hysteria
> during World War I, name changing became the rage. The Cincinnati
> City Council followed the trend by changing German Street names
> on April 9, 1918. Among those changed were: German Street to
> English Street, Bismarck Street to Montreal Street, Berlin Street to
> Woodrow Street, Bremen Street to Republic Street, Brunswick Street
> to Edgecliff Point, Frankfort Street to Connecticut Street, Hanover
> Street to Yukon Street, Hapsburg Street to Merimac Street,
> Schumann Street to Meredith Street, Vienna Street to Panama Street,
> and Humboldt Street to Taft Road.

1918—As a result of the war, the Americanization Executive Committee is formed, which opens the American House at the corner of Central Avenue and Bank Street, and aims to address the problem it describes as ethnic groups living like transplanted "European colonies in various sections of America, leading their isolated lives in a monotonous daily drudge . . . ," according to a pamphlet describing its work, *The Americanization Problem in Cincinnati* (1921).[28]

1919—A statewide law, later declared unconstitutional, prohibits German-language instruction in schools below the eighth grade. This law is later declared unconstitutional by the Supreme Court in 1923.

1919–32—Prohibition strikes an economic blow to the Over-the-Rhine district, which depends on the brewing trade, as well as restaurants and beer gardens, and from which it never recovered.

1920s—German-Americans continue moving throughout the city and region, but especially to the west side of town, further strengthening the east side/west side dimension to the city based on the German heritage.

Several new societies are formed in the 1920s, including the Kolping Society. The German Literary Club celebrates its fiftieth anniversary in 1927.

Many Germans immigrate in the 1920s due to the inflation, and also as a result of the breakup of the old Austro-Hungarian Empire. Among the immigrants is Christian Weishaupt who, by 1929, establishes his own general contracting firm, which supervises the building of the University of Cincinnati's Nippert Stadium and many Works Progress Administration (WPA) projects in the area. His company is to build so many sidewalks in the area, which are imprinted with his name, that he becomes known as the "Sidewalk King." He later serves as the last president of the German Pioneer Society.

1920—The Volstead Act goes into effect, and Prohibition lasts until 1933, giving rise to bootleggers, including German-Americans such as George Remus, who makes millions of dollars. Postwar relief is organized by the Society for the Needy Children of Central Europe, led by Howard Wurlitzer.

1921—Charles Schmidt, president of the German-American Combined Singers and national president of the North American Saengerbund, presents the main address at the annual meeting of the German Pioneer Society, stating that German heritage blended perfectly well with American patriotism, as demonstrated by the record of the German Pioneer Society, which held celebrations on the birthdays of Presidents Washington and Lincoln. Throughout the 1920s, he emphasizes that German-Americans should eliminate any misunderstandings relating to German-Americans that emanated from the First World War, and work on behalf of relations between the United States and Germany.

1929—In Cincinnati, there are 490 arrests for bootlegging, and the area is said to be honeycombed with home-brew parlors, speakeasies, and private clubs.

The first German-American radio program, *Eine Rheinreise*, was broadcast on WCKY, beginning the first of many German-American radio programs that will continue from this time.

Last appearance at the May Festival of Madam Ernestine Schumann-Heink, the world famous contralto, who sings almost annually at the festival from 1900 to 1914. She becomes especially well known by means of her Victrola recording of "Stille Nacht."

1930s—Refugees, especially German Jews, come to Cincinnati to escape the Third Reich. Arriving at age thirteen with his family in 1939 is Francis Loewenheim from Nuernberg. He attends the University of Cincinnati and Columbia University, and becomes a well-known historian at Rice University, often contributing editorial commentaries to the newspapers of Cincinnati. Included among his many books, is *Peace or Appeasement? Hitler, Chamberlain, and the Munich Crisis* (1965), which he edits. The Hebrew Union College starts the "Refugee Scholars Project" and succeeds in bringing eleven leading scholars to its Clifton campus in the 1930s and 1940s.

1933—Prohibition is repealed. In Cincinnati, Prohibition means the loss of the family-style beer gardens. After repeal, they are replaced by the dimly-lit taverns of a new day. Among the remaining pre-Prohibition establishments is Mecklenburg Gardens.

The 250th anniversary of the founding of Germantown, Pennsylvania, is celebrated at Emery Auditorium, with the main address deliv-

Charles G. Schmidt
Photo Courtesy of Peggy Schmidt.

ered by historian Albert B. Faust, who states that German-Americans "have had their share of failure and success, of trial and triumph, of labor and honest effort in the building of the American nation. They are privileged to love and cherish America as rightful partners, as owners in common with other great European stocks that compose the American people. The study of our history makes us better Americans, secure in traditions of service, true in devotion to national ideals."[29]

1934—Edwin H. Zeydel becomes head of the German Department at the University of Cincinnati, and serves until 1961. He not only establishes a national and international reputation for the department, but also publishes many books dealing with German literature, as well as textbooks for German instruction, such as *Mein Tagebuch: Graded Readings for Beginners in German* (1956). He also translates many works from German to English, including nonliterary works such as *A Refutation of the Versailles War Guilt Thesis* by Alfred von Wegerer (1930).

1938—German Day at Coney Island attracts thirty-eight thousand people.

1939—Fearing another war and the possibility of another anti-German crusade, the *Cincinnati Freie Presse* publishes "Our Platform for German-Americans," which proclaims "Absolute and unswerving loyalty to American ideals and principles," and "Continued and consistent efforts to inculcate that spirit in the mind and heart of every citizen of German extraction." It also pledges "Co-operation in the effort to uplift the social, cultural, and business life of Greater Cincinnati." Other points stressed are dedication to the "Advancement of Cincinnati's prestige as a music and art center; Development of spiritual virtues and closer cooperation with scriptural laws and edicts;" and "Promotion of a spirit of brotherly love and adherence to the Golden Rule."[30]

A Turner program also stresses patriotism: "What is Turnerism? Turnerism is a system of education, combining rational physical and mental development for the express purpose of strengthening the national power and fostering true patriotism—and true patriotism stands for the preservation of democracy and the attainment and maintenance of political, economic, religious, and personal liberty."[31]

1941–45—Due to anti-German sentiment, German-Americans are interned across the country during the Second World War, including well-known Cincinnati Germans such as Dr. Wilhelm Huebener, personal physician of the former Kaiser, Wilhelm II. Fortunately, Dr. Huebener is almost immediately released, which is the exception rather than the rule.

1943—Thomas Mann returns to Cincinnati for the second time to present a lecture here. Before his lecture in 1939, he said "My stay in Cincinnati, although unfortunately a very short one, is of special interest to me, among other reasons because of the fact that there is an important German colony living here, and I am sure that some members thereof will attend my lecture this evening. That will give me a particularly warm and comforting feeling because we Germans living outside the Reich feel ourselves to be just as good sons of Luther and Goethe as any living within the German boundaries, and today, because we are living in freedom, our opportunity to represent and to nurture true Germandom may be even greater."[32] During his 1943 lecture, he commented on relations between Germany and America, and the role he and others could play. He felt that in the future a bridge would draw both countries closer together, and that this bridge consisted of the large group of German immigrants and exiles who had come to America, and that they would contribute not only to United States–Germany relations, but to the postwar reconstruction of Germany.

1949–51—Concordia Lutheran Church assists about 125 recently-arrived German immigrants with getting settled, including helping them to get furniture and basic household items. Members of the church also help them become accustom to their new homes, find jobs for them, provide transportation, etc. Many other churches do the same in assisting recently-arrived German immigrants in the postwar period.

1950s—Immigration of ethnic Germans from southeast Europe known as the Donauschwaben, and who, in 1956, sponsor the first Danube Swabian Day.

1950—The German-American Combined Singers sponsor a concert at Music Hall for the relief of postwar Germany, which adds to the considerable funds collected by the local German-American Relief for Germany Committee.

1952–1955—The Forty-first National Saengerfest of the North American Saengerbund is held in Cincinnati, as is the National Song Festival of the Federation of German-American Workers' Singing Societies. Walter C. Langsam becomes president of the University of Cincinnati, and will serve until 1971. A well-known historian of many works dealing with European history, including his *The World Since 1914*, which went through eight editions, Langsam later publishes a volume dealing with the region, *Cincinnati in Color* (1978). In 1970, he receives the Order of Merit of the Federal Republic of Germany for his contributions to German-American relations.

1958—German-American Week is proclaimed by the City of Cincinnati, reflecting the re-emergence of pride in the German heritage.

1968—The Tri-State German-American School Society is formed to offer German instructional classes in a Saturday school program.

1969—The four area breweries are Hudepohl, Burger, Schoenling, and Wiedemann.

1971—The Germania Society, founded in 1964, pioneers the first Oktoberfest in Cincinnati.

1974—The Fairview German Language School, the only German bilingual public school in Ohio, opens, and returns German instruction to the elementary school level for the first time since World War I.

The German-Americana Collection, one of the largest collections of its kind, is established at the University of Cincinnati. It is based on the private library of Dr. H. H. Fick, formerly superintendent of the German Department of the Cincinnati Public Schools before World War I.

1975—Three German societies celebrate their centennial at German Day at Kolping Grove.

1976—The first Oktoberfest Zinzinnati is held in Downtown Cincinnati in honor of the German heritage during the American Bicentennial year, and the Public Library of Cincinnati and Hamilton County sponsors an exhibit on the German heritage entitled "Prosit Cincinnati," with a guide that states "The Germans that have been arriving since 1788 have impressed a distinct Teutonic flavor on the Queen of the West, which has enriched this beautiful inland community and become inculcated forever into its milieu."[33]

German Day at Kolping Grove has its highest attendance in decades, with an attendance of more than ten thousand.

1980s—MainStrasse German Village is created in Covington, Kentucky.

1982—Local German newspaper, the *Cincinnati Kurier*, is acquired by the *Amerika-Woche*, published in Chicago. Later, the newspaper will be published in New York and will continue to carry regional news.

1983—Celebration of the German-American Tricentennial, the three-hundredth anniversary of the founding of the first German settlement in America at Germantown, Pennsylvania. A year-long program of activities, events, lectures, exhibits, and more, takes place.

1987—The German-American Studies Program is established at the University of Cincinnati, which is the only one in the United States that offers a certificate in German-American Studies.

First celebration of National German-American Day on 6 October, which comes about as a result of a national campaign initiated by the Society for German-American Studies, and led by its president, Don Heinrich Tolzmann, University of Cincinnati. President Ronald Reagan's proclamation for German-American Day stated:

> More Americans trace their heritage back to German ancestry than to any other nationality. More than seven million Germans have come to our shores through the years, and today some 60 million Americans—one in four—are of German descent. Few people have blended so completely into the multicultural tapestry of American society and yet have made such singular economic, political, social, scientific, and cultural contributions to the growth and success of these United States as have Americans of German extraction.
>
> The United States has embraced a vast array of German traditions, institutions and influences. Many of these have become so accepted as parts of our way of life that their ethnic origin has become obscured. For instance, Christmas trees and Broadway musicals are familiar features of American society. Our kindergartens, graduate schools, the social security system, and labor unions are all based on models derived from Germany.

Don Heinrich Tolzmann and President Ronald Reagan at the signing ceremony in the White House Rose Garden for the proclamation of the first celebration of National German-American Day on October 6, 1987.

German teachers, musicians, and enthusiastic amateurs have left an indelible imprint on classical music, hymns, choral singing, and marching bands in our country. In architecture and design, German contributions include the modern suspension bridge, Bauhaus, and Jugendstil. German-American scientists have helped make the United States the world's pioneer in research and technology. The American work ethic, a major factor in the rapid rise of the United States to preeminence in agriculture and industry, owes much to German-Americans' commitment to excellence. For more than three centuries, Germans have helped build, invigorate, and strengthen this country. But the United States has given as well as received. Just a generation ago, America conceived of and swiftly implemented the Marshall Plan, which helped the new German democracy rise from the rubble of war to become a beacon of democracy in Central Europe. The Berlin Airlift demonstrated the American commitment to the defense of freedom when, still recovering from war, Berlin was threatened by strangulation from the Soviets.

Reagan went on to say:

Germans and Americans are rightfully proud of our common values as well as our shared heritage. For more than three decades the German-American partnership has been a linchpin in the Western Alliance. Thanks to it, a whole generation of Americans and Europeans has grown up free to enjoy the fruits of liberty.

Our liberties are thus intertwined. We now contribute to each other's trade, enjoy each other's cultures, and learn from each other's experiences. The German-American Friendship Garden . . . in the District of Columbia…is symbolic of the close and amicable relations" between Germany and America." He closed in urging all Americans to learn more about German-American contributions "to the life and culture of the United States and to observe this day with appropriate ceremonies and activities.[34]

Since 1987, German-American Day has been celebrated annually on a national basis on 6 October.

1988—H. A. Rattermann-Strasse is officially dedicated in Ankum, Germany, the home town of Cincinnati's prolific German-American historian. Visitors to Ankum, located near Osnabrueck, may visit the town's historical museum, which features an exhibit of the works of Rattermann. Also on display is a telephone directory of Cincinnati, which is of interest, as so many people emigrated from the area to Cincinnati.

1989—Sister-city relationship is established with Munich, with Auguste Kent as the driving force behind the effort, which reaches back to the 1950s.

The German-American Heritage Month, pioneered in Cincinnati, is now a national celebration.

1990—Celebration of the unification of Germany as part of the German-American Heritage Month: the Day of German Unity takes place on 3 October, and German-American Day takes place on 6 October.

1993—After the seventy-fifth anniversary of the First World War, the German-American Studies Program, in cooperation with the Ohio Historical Society, dedicates a historical marker, located in the Fairview Park in Clifton Heights, that is entitled "Anti-German Hysteria," and commemorates the wrongs and injustices against the German heritage that took place during the war. See the entry under the date of 1918 for the text of the marker.

Franziska C. Ott publishes *Cincinnati German Imprints: A Checklist*, which lists more than fourteen hundred German-language books printed in Cincinnati since 1826, clearly demonstrating that Cincinnati was one of the major centers of German-American book publishing.

1995—One Hundredth Annual German Day celebration in Cincinnati at the Germania Park. At the request of the German-American Citizens League, the City of Cincinnati installs informational signs at twelve streets that had German names before World War I. The informational signs read as follows, for example: "Formerly Bremen St., renamed April 2, 1918," because of the anti-German hysteria.

1996—Appointment of Richard Erich Schade, Professor of German at the University of Cincinnati, as Honorary German Consul for the region. Schade also serves as editor of the *Lessing Yearbook*. Germany has had an unbroken line of consular representatives since the 1850s.

1997—Establishment of the Max Kade German Cultural Center at the University of Cincinnati, where programs, conferences, lectures, etc. are held.

The Twenty-first Century

2000—Grand opening of the German Heritage Museum at West Fork Park, which aims to showcase the German heritage of the region.

The 125th anniversary of the Bavarian Beneficial Society, which was founded to support members in sickness and their survivors in case of death, as well as to further the German heritage.

2001—In cooperation with the German-American Citizens League, the Ohio Bicentennial Commission dedicates a historical marker honoring "Cincinnati's German Heritage" at Sawyer Point on the Ohio River in Cincinnati.

2002—New newspaper appears, *German-American Chronicle of the Ohio Valley*, replacing the newsletter, *German-American News*, which had appeared since 1995, and which circulates throughout the region providing news and information regarding the German heritage. Rogar Schneider serves as news editor. Marge Poole becomes the next editor of the newsletter which, in 2006, changes its name to *German-American News* once again.

2003—The Hofbraeuhaus Newport is dedicated in Newport, Kentucky, and is the place outside of Munich, Germany, where fresh HB beer can be obtained. Four of the beers served are brewed on site, with a fifth imported from Munich, where the Hofbraeuhaus was founded in 1589 by Duke Wilhelm V of Bavaria. Its menu includes a local favorite: Glier's goetta links from Covington.

In an interview with the *Cincinnati Post* (2 May 2003), Erich Kunzel, conductor of the Cincinnati Pops Orchestra, comments on the 125th anniversary of the Music Hall, noting that the Hall is "in a sense the history of Cincinnati," and that it all began with Germans in the Over-the-Rhine district. "A lot of hard-working Germans came to

Hofbraeuhaus Newport in Newport, Kentucky.

Beer Garden at Hofbrauhaus in Newport, Kentucky.

Cincinnati in the nineteenth century and settled in Over-the-Rhine. They were famous for their breweries, their beer halls and their singing. When Conductor Theodore Thomas came to Cincinnati to start a May Festival, he noticed that the Germans, who loved to sing, were situated in Over-the-Rhine. So when he asked the city to build a hall for the May Festival, it was decided, hey, let's not build it downtown, let's build it where the singers are." The Music Hall, therefore, serves as another lasting and vital influence of the German heritage in the region.

German-American radio programs are available in the area, with Heinz Probst's *Over-the-Rhine Showcase* Program and Hans Kroschke's *German Tunes of the Queen City*, both providing German music and community news and announcements weekly. Also, Cincinnati maintains its reputation as the city of festivals, with 130 fests taking place from June through October each year. More than half are sponsored by area churches and the rest by societies, organizations, and communities.

This year marks the seventy-fifth anniversary of Lunken Airport. Edmund Lunkenheimer, the son of German-born Frederick Lunkenheimer who founded the Lunkenheimer Company, maker of valves, donated 230 acres of land near Kellogg Avenue to be used for the development of a municipal airport. In appreciation, the airport was named after Edmund who had changed his name to Lunken.

On December 16, 2003, an Ohio Historical Bicentennial Marker was dedicated at 2701 Spring Grove Avenue in honor of the "First Glass Door Oven," with the marker's text stating: "The first full-size glass door oven was invented and manufactured here by Ernst H. Huenefeld of the Huenefeld Company in 1909." *The Cincinnati Post* noted, "we take it for granted today the ability to peer through the oven door to see how the pie is doing. But back then the ability to monitor food in the oven without opening the door was one of those household breakthroughs that people were eager to get. . . . Huenefeld, who died in 1931 at the age of 92, was more than a successful entrepreneur. He was among the group that incorporated Bethesda Hospital in 1896, contributed heavily to German Methodist causes in Ohio, and in 1908 donated his Clifton estate to Bethesda for use as a retirement home—the one we know today as Scarlet Oaks." Huenefeld, born in 1838 in Ladbergen, near Bremen, immigrated in 1845 to Ohio.

The Ohio Historical Bicentennial Marker that honors the "First Glass Door Oven" is located at 2701 Spring Grove Avenue.

Advertisement for Glass Door Oven

Huenefeld Company

2004—The Christian Moerlein Brewing Company was brought back to life by Gregory Hardman and in 2007, the company opened its OTR Ale Haus on Elder Street in the Over-the-Rhine district, just north of Findlay Market.

2005—The 110th German Day celebration takes place, one of the oldest celebrations of its kind in the United States.

2006—The 200th anniversary of the birth of John A. Roebling who designed the Suspension Bridge on the Ohio River. Renovation of the bridge begins in November.

The John A. Roebling Suspension Bridge on the Ohio River.
Photograph with permission of Stevie Publishing/Robert W. Stevie.

CHAPTER 2

GERMAN HERITAGE HIGHLIGHTS

THERE ARE MANY ASPECTS of the German heritage that stand forth and are particularly noteworthy, but which would require a lengthier volume to do justice to. However, some representative examples are provided here, as they demonstrate the extent to which the German heritage has become an integral part of the region.[1]

Martin Baum

Martin Baum is considered the father of the German immigrations not only to Cincinnati, but to the entire Ohio Valley region as well. He came to Cincinnati in 1795, and became one of the wealthiest citizens as a merchant, banker, and real estate agent. He owned a foundry, the first sugar refinery, and held investments in steamboats. Through his agents stationed at New Orleans, Baltimore, and Philadelphia, he attracted German immigrants to Cincinnati to work in his businesses, thus acquiring for Cincinnati the reputa-

Martin Baum

tion as a destination for German immigrants. Baum and his family came from Hagenau in Alsace-Lorraine. Today, his former home is the Taft Museum of Art. Baum was elected twice to serve as mayor of Cincinnati (1807, 1812), and played a leading role in the early cultural life of Cincinnati.

David Ziegler

David Ziegler

What city has a German-born veteran of the American Revolution as its first Mayor? Cincinnati, of course! Born in Heidelberg in 1748, Ziegler served in the Prussian and Russian armies, before coming to America in 1774. After the Battle of Lexington, he joined the War for Independence, and advanced to Commissary General of the Department of Pennsylvania. After the Revolution, he was stationed at western forts, finally to Fort Washington in Cincinnati. In the military Ziegler was "always considered the first in point of discipline and appearance." During the first two years after the incorporation of the town of Cincinnati in 1802, Ziegler was elected president, or mayor, of the city council. He also served as the first marshal of the Ohio district and adjutant general of Ohio in 1807 and, at the time of his death in 1811, was the surveyor of the port of Cincinnnati. A plaque in his honor is at the Memorial Hall in the Over-the-Rhine district.

The Waldschmidt House

The Waldschmidt House, located in Camp Dennison, is today a museum maintained by the Ohio Daughters of the American Revolution. It was part of a settlement known as "Germany," established there in 1795–6 by Christian Waldschmidt and a group of Pennsylvania German pietists. At this site, Waldschmidt erected the first paper mill in Ohio, and the buildings are the oldest in Hamilton County. Most likely, the first German religious services and the first German instructional classes were held here. The buildings at Germany were constructed of fieldstone and resemble those found in the Pennsylvania German homeland of the settlers.

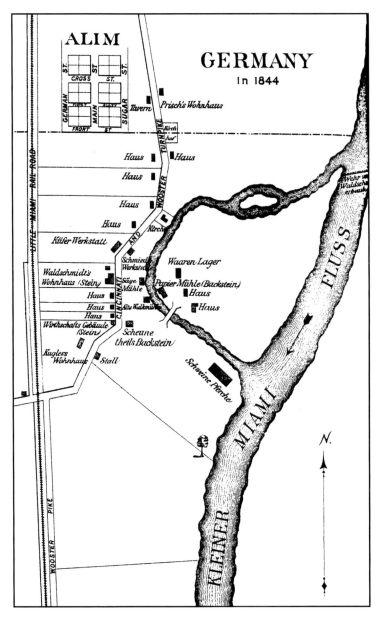

Map of Germany, Ohio, now known as Camp Dennison.

Over-the-Rhine

A section known as Over-the-Rhine, an area of 213 acres, became the nineteenth-century locale of the German-American community. Its borders were defined by the Miami-Erie Canal, now Central Parkway, on the west and south; on the east, by Reading Road and Liberty; and on the north by McMicken Avenue. The old barge canal, completed in 1831, was dubbed the "Rhine," because when one crossed over it, one entered the German district. According to one commentator, in Over-the-Rhine "everything is German and even the American discards his formality and envelops himself in German Gemuetlichkeit." The district was noted for "neat little frame and brick houses built flush with the sidewalk, and with backyards fenced in with lattice work and planted with flower and vegetable gardens." See chapter 4 for a guide to historic sites in the Over-the-Rhine district.[2]

"Over-the-Rhine"

German-American Societies

Cincinnati's first German society, or Verein, was founded in 1819 and, since that time, hundreds more have been formed. They serve a wide variety of purposes and functions: social, cultural, political, fraternal, literary, historical, philanthropic, etc. Today, there are twenty German societies in the Greater Cincinnati area, which are affiliated with the German-American Citizens League, the umbrella organization for regional societies. Formed in 1895, the League has recently established the German Heritage Museum, located in West Fork Park, in Green Township, to showcase and illuminate the German heritage of the region.

Cincinnati German Barbers in Reichrath Park, circa 1900. From the Barber's Local Union, collection US-86-15, Archives and Rare Books, University of Cincinnati.

German Singing Societies

In 1849, German singing societies from Louisville, Indiana, and Cincinnati met here to hold their first Saengerfest, or songfest. At the same time, they established the German-American Federation of Singing Societies, which celebrated its 150th anniversary in Cincinnati in 1999 at the Kolping Society. The Saengerfest tradition was incorporated into the May Festival in 1873, and in 1988 a Saengerfest was held at the Music Hall as part of Cincinnati's Bicentennial. Today's Kolping Saengerchor continues the tradition of Cincinnati's German-American singing societies.

Old Saint Mary's Church

Located at 123 East Thirteenth Street in Over-the-Rhine, Old Saint Mary's was built in 1841 by German Catholics and is unique from all local churches, since the bricks were baked in the ovens of the parishioners, and is, therefore, a homemade church. The church features paintings from Germany, and beautiful stained glass windows with German inscriptions, such as "Maria bitt fuer uns," or "Maria, pray for us." A German Mass is held weekly.

Mother of God Church

Located at 119 West Sixth Street in Covington, this church was built by German Catholics in 1870/71 with funds from the Leopoldine Mission Society of Vienna. Considered one of the most beautiful German-American churches in the area, it contains five murals by Johann Schmitt, who trained Frank Duveneck, and has stained glass windows from Munich. It also contains paintings and sculptures by other German-American artists. The organ, installed in 1876, was made by A. Koehnken and Grimm, and is considered one of the finest in the country.

Friedrich Jahn Memorial Monument

Located on a hillside terrace in Inwood Park on Vine Street is the Jahn Memorial Monument dedicated to Friedrich Jahn (1778–1852), who established the first Turnverein, or Turner society, in Berlin in 1811. The motto of the Turners was "a sound mind in a sound body," and they fought in the wars of liberation against Napoleon, and also in the 1848 Revolution in Germany. This Memorial was dedicated by the Cincinnati Turnverein, which was founded in 1848 by refugees of the 1848 Revolution. It was created by the well-known German-American sculptor Leopold Fettweis (1848–1912), who created many other works of sculpture in the area. Carved in relief on the surface of the granite is a broken trunk of an oak tree and an inscription honoring the Turnvater, or father of the Turner Movement.

Friedrich Hecker Monument

Created by German-American sculptor Leopold Fettweis (1848–1912), this marble monument, located in Washington Park in the Over-the-Rhine district, pays tribute to Friedrich Hecker (1811–1881), one of the leaders of the 1848 Revolution in Germany. He came to Cincinnati in 1848 and helped found the Cincinnati Turnverein, the first Turner society in America. Hecker later joined the Union Army and served as a brigadier general. The German inscription on the monument is translated as follows: "With Word and Deed for the Freedom of the People in the Old and New Fatherlands."

Friedrich Hassaurek

Friedrich Hassaurek was a Forty-eighter who came to America from Vienna after participating in the 1848 Revolution there. He became an influential editor of the Cincinnati Volksblatt, the major German-American newspaper in Cincinnati. He strongly supported the Republican crusade against slavery. In 1860, he served as a delegate to the Republican convention in Chicago, and played an important role in the election for Lincoln, campaigning across the Midwest in German-American communities.

German-American Regiments in the Civil War

Four of the seven regiments formed in Cincinnati during the Civil War were German-American, but the most well known was the Ninth Ohio Regiment. Four days after Lincoln's call for volunteers, the Ninth was formed. It needed one thousand men, and more than two thousand applied. Most were members of the Cincinnati Turnverein, founded in 1848 by refugees of the 1848 Revolution in Germany. A local paper wrote of the unit: "The first company of Turner men were as solid as heart pine and as supple as antelopes. They passed the examination ordeal solidly and lost not a man. As the army surgeon struck their chests they sounded like so many anvils." The regiment played a crucial role at several battles, but took heavy casualties, and when it mustered out, only half of the regiment had survived. Robert E. Lee was reputed to have said that without the German-American soldiers in the Union Army that the South "could whip the Yankees easily."

Turner Hall

August von Willich

Called the "military father" of the Civil War's Ninth Ohio Regiment from Cincinnati, August von Willich was better known to his soldiers as "Papa Willich." Born in 1812 in East Prussia, he joined the Potsdam Military Academy at age twelve and continued his education at the Royal Military Academy in Berlin, after which he became an officer in the Prussian Army. After participating in the failed 1848 Revolution in Germany, he came to Cincinnati in 1853, edited a German newspaper, volunteered for service at age forty-nine when the Civil War broke out, and became adjutant of the Ninth Regiment. Later, he was called to organize another German-American regiment, the Thirty-second Indiana. He fought at more than thirty battles, including Shiloh, Perryville, Missionary Ridge, and Chickamauga, until 1863 when a bullet wound put him out of action, whereupon he became commander of the military district of Cincinnati.

Spring Grove Cemetery

In 1855, Prussian-born Adolph Strauch became Superintendent of Spring Grove Cemetery and initiated a comprehensive landscaping plan that became world famous. He first settled in Cincinnati to develop and care for the hilltop estates of families, such as the Probasco in Clifton. Spring Grove Cemetery is a beautiful park and nature preserve, especially in the spring when the tulips are in bloom surrounded by flowering trees and shrubs. Spring Grove serves as a biographical directory of the city's past "movers and shakers," who are honored by artfully designed monuments of high-grade stones, such as

Adolph Strauch

marble and granite in a natural setting. Strauch acquired his landscaping skills in Germany and Austria, and was one of the many German-Americans who contributed to the Queen City of the West.

The Roebling Suspension Bridge

Completed in 1867, the Roebling Suspension Bridge is a veritable symbol of the entire Greater Cincinnati area and connects Covington and Cincinnati. It is considered Roebling's model for his world-famous Brooklyn Bridge. Widely viewed as an architectural and historic landmark, it is also considered symbolic of the area and of what an immigrant could accomplish in the New World. Measuring 1,057 feet between the 230-foot-high towers and 1,619 feet between the shore anchors, it cost $1.8 million to build. It was placed on the National Register of Historic Places in 1975 and illuminated with lights in 1984 in honor of Julia Langsam, who served as president of the Covington and Cincinnati Bridge Company.

Fountain Square

The centerpiece of Cincinnati, The Tyler Davidson Fountain serves as the symbol of the city. Cast by Ferdinand von Miller, the fountain was designed by August von Kreling. It was donated to the city in 1871 by Henry Probasco, and dedicated on 6 October, which became German-American Day. The forty-three-foot-high fountain contains thirteen allegorical figures and four bas-reliefs depicting the blessings of water for mankind, with the central figure, the Genius of Water, standing with outstretched arms showering water from her hands.

Andrew Erkenbrecher

Andrew Erkenbrecher established the only starch factory in the world where wooden apparatus were entirely replaced by those of stone. His starch factory was unique with its immense tank of stone and cement. By the 1870s, his company was manufacturing close to forty thousand pounds of starch daily. Erkenbrecher was a Bavarian who came to America at age fourteen in 1836 and, within several years, commenced his highly successful business career. His civic pursuits were many, chief among them being the founding of the Cincinnati Zoo. In 1872, a larva was stripping trees of

Andrew Erkenbrecher

their foliage, so he set up a Society for the Acclimatization of Birds, and imported thousands of birds from Europe, in the hope they would rid the city of the pesky caterpillar. Out of his interest in birds emerged the idea for the Cincinnati Zoo.

Frank Duveneck

Located at 1226 Greenup Street in Covington, this was the home of Frank Duveneck (1848–1919), considered the premier artist of the region. After having been apprenticed to Covington's Institute of Catholic Art, he went to Munich in 1869, where he studied at the Royal Academy of Fine Arts. After living in various places in Europe and America, he accepted a position in 1900 at the Art Academy of Cincinnati, and attracted a sizable following of students. He was considered the greatest painter of his generation, and may very well have been the greatest German-American artist from the area.

Musical Influences

German-Americans greatly influenced the musical life of Cincinnati. In 1867, Clara Baur, a pianist and singer, founded the Conservatory of Music, based on the Stuttgarter Hochschule fuer Musik. The College of Music, established in 1878, was directed by Theodore Thomas from Hannover. German influences are most apparent in the development of the May Festival and the Cincinnati Symphony Orchestra. Local German-American singing societies helped organize the first May Festival in 1873, which was directed by Thomas, and the Cincinnati Symphony Orchestra consisted largely of German-American musicians, who played in orchestras in Over-the-Rhine.

Heinrich A. Rattermann

A German Horatio Alger, Heinrich Rattermann rose from slaughterhouse worker to wealthy businessman, historian, and poet. He was born in Ankum near Osnabrueck, Germany. Arriving in Cincinnati in 1846, he later founded the German Mutual Insurance Company (now the Hamilton Mutual Insurance Company), located in the Germania Building on Walnut Street in Over-the-Rhine. He also helped organize the May Festival, and was active in founding German-American singing societies. He edited Der Deutsche Pionier (The German Pioneer), a valuable German-American historical journal, and helped organize the first German Day in Cincinnati in 1895, which led to the formation of the German-American Citizens League, which still sponsors German Day. Rattermann's longest poem was Vater Rhein, or Father Rhine, whose romantic flavor is indicated by the following excerpt:

> German Rhine, so rich in legendary lore, I challenge you to proclaim the glorious thoughts which animate you on your meandering journey. Your verdant shores abound in noble deeds; at your fountains bards and heroes imbibe their inspirations. Speak then, O Stream, with open mind, of noble deeds and wonders great, of daring courage and success, while your admirer lounge at the goblets of fiery wine. . . .

Musical influences. First generation German-American ladies. Descendants from the Kitt family of Hayna, Germany.

German Influences in Business & Industry

German-Americans have played a major role in business and industry, especially in the meat and meat packing industries, the food industry, the machine industry, the building trades, banking and finance, and, of course, brewing. Local banking grew largely out of the building and loan associations, or Bauvereine. So many bakers in Cincinnati were German that they formed their own singing society. Perhaps the easiest way to gauge the German-American impact is to page through the German surnames in the telephone directory.

Christian Moerlein

Christian Moerlein, before coming to America in 1842, was a blacksmith and farmer, who learned the brewing trade in his native town of Truppach in Bavaria. In Cincinnati, he began brewing in 1853, and in 1855–56 formed a partnership with Conrad Windisch. Within ten years the company had brewed ten thousand barrels. Ten years later, he bought out Windisch. By 1872, the Moerlein Brewery employed eighty workers, and by 1889, was producing 350,000 barrels annually and was the largest brewery in Cincinnati. Moerlein's Brewery was considered a premium beer and prospered until Prohibition. It made a brief appearance again after Repeal in 1933.

The Hauck House

Located at 812 Dayton Street, this home belonged to the well-known Cincinnati German brewer John Hauck, who brewed one of Cincinnati's finest beers. It is now a museum known as the Hauck House, and contains exhibits and displays of the family and the pre-Prohibition era. Among the beers produced were John Hauck Golden Eagle Lager, Export Lager, SuperFine, Pilsner, and Invalid Beer—the latter for the improvement of the health of the weak and sickly! John Hauck also served as president of the German National Bank in downtown Cincinnati.

Ohios Muster=Brauerei

Ihre Bestimmungen, Maschinerie und ihr Produkt
haben den höchsten Punkt der **Vollkommenheit**
erreicht und stehen ohne Konkurrenz da.

THE JOHN HAUCK BREWING CO.

Cincinnati, O.

Unsere Marken, Faß= und Flaschenbier:

„Golden Eagle". „Imperial".

„Special Dark",

gebraut von **feinstem Malz** und **auserlesenstem Hopfen**,
übertreffen alle anderen Produkte dieser Art.

World War I

Due to the anti-German hysteria of World War I, the Cincinnati City Council passed an ordinance changing German street names. Among those changed were: German Street to English Street; Berlin Street to Woodrow Street; Schumann Street to Meredith Street; and Humboldt Street to Taft Road. A historical marker in Fairview Heights Park commemorates these street name changes, and also records that "In Cincinnati, German teachers were dismissed from public schools, German professors were censored, German collections and publications were removed from circulation from the Public Library, businesses with German names had their names 'Americanized,' and by police order, only English language meetings could be held."

The German National Bank

Located at 2 West Fourth Street, the German National Bank was forced to change its name to the Lincoln National Bank during the First World War due to the anti-German hysteria, as did many banks and businesses in the area. However, the inscription with the original name is clearly visible today, an indication that the German heritage is an integral part of the landscape here.

German Restaurants and Bakeries

Mecklenburg Gardens is a historic restaurant with a German-style Biergarten, which was built in 1865. Located in Corryville, Mecklenburg's became a favorite gathering place for meeting and relaxation in the nineteenth century. Practice elections were also held there to acquaint German immigrants with the American

Mecklenburg Gardens

political process. Before Prohibition there were countless beer gardens in Cincinnati, and Mecklenburg's, fortunately, is one that survived that era and symbolizes a popular part of the German heritage.

In the 1880s Christian Moerlein built a home at 151 West McMillan as a wedding gift for his daughter, who married John Goetz. In 1955, Lenhardt's Restaurant was opened on McMillan Avenue, and in 1965, was moved into the Goetz house. In 1990, the Lenhardt's granddaughter, Christy Windholtz, took over the business, continuing the fine traditions

Lenhardt's Restaurant

of the restaurant, which opened a Biergarten in 1998.

Wertheims's Restaurant

Other German restaurants in the area are the Black Forest Restaurant of George Fraundorfer in Cincinnati and Wertheim's Restaurant of Sal Wertheim in Covington. Among bakeries, Servatii's, which has several stores throughout the area, is well known for its German-style breads and pastries.

Oldenburg, Indiana

Where can you find street signs in German in the region? Not just German names, but in the German language? In Oldenburg, Indiana! Located just west of Cincinnati is a town founded by German immigrants from the Oldenburg region of northern Germany. They first came to Cincinnati, which was not only the destination point, but also the distribution center for German immigrants throughout the region. Other villages and towns in the region were founded by Germans who came through Cincinnati, including New Alsace in Indiana and, north of Cincinnati, Minster, which sponsors an annual Oktoberfest.

MainStrasse Village

The Main-Strasse Village, located on the west side of Covington, was established in the 1970s and aimed to restore housing and establish a business district there. All were developed with a German heritage motif due to northern Kentucky's substantial German-American population. Many specialty stores, restaurants, and gift shops filled the charming village, which includes several points of interest. The Goose Girl Fountain, for example, is based on a German fairy tale by the famous Grimm Brothers, "The Goose Girl." Goebel Park, located on the west end of the Village, honors William Goebel, a German-American elected governor of Kentucky in 1900. The park features a Glockenspiel, dedicated in 1979, known as the Carroll Chimes Bell Tower, honoring then Governor Julian Carroll of Kentucky. The German Gothic Glockenspiel plays a forty-three-bell carillon hourly to present mini-concerts and the lively enactment of German folklore, such as "The Pied Piper of Hamelin." See chapter 5 for a guide to historic sites in Covington.

Glockenspiel at Goebel Park in MainStrasse Village

The Fairview German School

Located in Clifton Heights, this elementary school had been a German bilingual school before the First World War. But German instruction was eliminated from the curriculum due to the anti-German hysteria of the time. In 1974, German was finally returned to the public schools at the elementary level for the first time since the First World War, and Fairview has earned a reputation as one of the best such schools in the nation.

Oktoberfest

Oktoberfest in Munich is the world's largest festival, and where does the second largest Oktoberfest take place? In Cincinnati, of course! Munich's sixteen-day fest begins officially when the Buergermeister taps the first barrel of beer, and concludes with the first Sunday in October. In like manner, Cincinnati's downtown Oktoberfest begins when Cincinnati's Buergermeister replicates the custom each mid-September on Fountain Square for a weekend of Gemuetlichkeit. The roots of Oktoberfest go back to a wedding celebration held in 1810 for Crown Prince Ludwig of Bavaria and Princess Therese of Saxe-Hildburghausen. In 1811, an agricultural show was added, and by 1818, booths and beer tents were added. Opening ceremonies and the procession were introduced in 1835 during the silver wedding anniversary of the Crown Prince and Princess. Cincinnati began the celebration in 1976.

German-American Heritage Month

German-American Heritage Month is celebrated nationally during October, and is centered on 6 October. On that day in 1683 the first permanent German settlement was founded at Germantown, Pennsylvania. In 1987, President Reagan and Congress declared 6 October a national day of commemoration, and in 1989, German-American Heritage Month was first proclaimed and celebrated.

The Lunkenheimer Company

The Lunkenheimer Company, founded in 1862 by Frederick Lunkenheimer, a German-born machinist, is one of Cincinnati's oldest companies and continues operations at its Fairmount location. Early on it became one of the leading manufacturers of specialized valves, including whistles, which were in great demand for use with steam engines. Although it still produces them, its major focus is now on valves. Today it is known as the Cincinnati Valve Company, a licensee of Lunkenheimer Valves. This company is a good example of how Germans contributed to the machine industry and provided jobs for

Lunkenheimer's Brass Foundry

legions of workers, while gaining Cincinnati a reputation as a national center for the machine industry.

Lunken Airport

Frederick Lunkenheimer's sons, Edmund and Eshelby, were interested in the new field of aviation and began to produce valves for use in airplanes. Charles Lindbergh used the products of the Lunkenheimer Company in his *Spirit of St. Louis*. After learning of the need for a municipal airport, Edmund donated 230 acres of land near Kellogg Avenue to the city to be used for aviation purposes. Lunken Airport is named in honor of Edmund Lunkenheimer who, in 1892, shortened his name to Lunken. Today, this airport is a busy hub for private and corporate aircraft.

CHAPTER 3

GERMAN HERITAGE
WHO'S WHO

T HOSE OF GERMAN DESCENT have made significant contributions to the Greater Cincinnati area in just about every field of
endeavor. The following selective list provides some examples of the
kinds of contributions they have made to the social, economic, political and cultural life of the area. Some of their names are well known
and require little or no explanation. Others may be not so well known,
but their contributions are nonetheless significant.[1]

Chris Ahrens—Founded the Ahrens Manufacturing Company, one
of the first builders of steam fire engines.

Martin Baum—Father of German immigration to the region, whose
former home is the Taft Museum of Art today.

Clara Baur—Founded the Conservatory of Music, based on the
model of the Stuttgarter Hochschule fuer Musik, which became the
forerunner of the University of Cincinnati's College Conservatory of
Music.

Robert F. Blum—Well-known Cincinnati-born German-American
artist.

Doris Kappelhoff Day—Well-known actress, who got her start in
Cincinnati, and whose father, Wilhelm Kappelhoff, was the director
of Cincinnati German-American singing societies.

Frank Duveneck—Premier German-American artist of the region.

Friedrich Eckstein—First German artist in Cincinnati, who
founded the Academy of Fine Art in the 1820s.

Andrew Erkenbrecher—The driving force behind the establishment
of the Cincinnati Zoo and Botanical Garden.

Doris Kappelhoff Day
Photograph by Jack Klumpe, courtesy of
University of Cincinnati Libraries.

Leopold Fettweis—German-American sculptor, whose works are found as monuments in area parks.

H. H. Fick—Head of the German Department of the Cincinnati Public Schools before World War I, which was one of the nation's finest programs, and whose private library became the foundation for the German-Americana Collection at the University of Cincinnati.

Julius Fleischmann—Nineteenth businessman with Fleischmann Yeast Company, who served as mayor of Cincinnati.

Gottfried and Johann Peter Frankenstein—Two early painters in Cincinnati, of whom especially the latter was well known.

Frederick A. Geier—Founder of Cincinnati Millacron, Inc.

William Goebel—First German-American governor of Kentucky for whom Goebel Park is named in the MainStrasse German Village in Covington.

Louis C. Graeter—Founding father of Graeter's ice cream business, which is well known for its outstanding quality.

Dr. H. H. Fick
Photograph from the German-Americana Collection,
University of Cincinnati.

Friedrich Hassaurek—A Forty-eighter, as refugees of the 1848 Revolution were known, who played an important role in regional politics, and who edited German-American newspapers and published volumes of prose and poetry.

John Hauck—Established the Hauck brewing company, considered one of Cincinnati's finest brews, and whose home is today's Hauck House Museum. His son, Dr. Frederick Hauck, was also well known as a scientist, businessman, and philanthropist.

John Hauck

John Hauser, Cincinnati German Artist
Photograph courtesy of the German-Americana Collection,
University of Cincinnati

John Hauser—German-American artist known for his scenes from the Wild West.

Joseph Anton Hemann—The first bilingual public school in the United States was organized by Hemann in 1840, when he opened the German-English School in Cincinnati, and also holds the honor of being the first public school teacher of German in America. He also served as principal of the school for the Old St. Mary's Church, and published German-American newspapers, including *Der Wahrheits-Freund* and *Der Volksfreund*. His home at 49 West McMillan is on the National Register of Historic Places.

August Herrmann—A member of the Boss Cox machine that ran Cincinnati before World War I. Hermann also owned the Cincinnati Reds.

Henry Holtgrewe—(1862–1917) was born in Hanover, Germany. As a saloon operator in Cincinnati, he entertained customers with his feats of strength, earning him the moniker, Cincinnati Strong Man..

Henry Holtgrewe—Cincinnati Strong Man

Ludwig Hudepohl

Ludwig Hudepohl—Established one of the major beer brewing companies in the history of Cincinnati.

Dr. Wilhelm Huebener—Prominent physician who served as the personal doctor to the former Kaiser, Wilhelm II, during his exile at Doorn, Holland.

Ernst H. Huenefeld—Born in 1838 in Ladbergen, Germany, near Bremen and immigrated to Ohio in 1845. He invented and manufactured the first successful full-size glass door oven at his Huenefeld Company in 1909.

Elias Kahn—Founder of a major meat-packing company in Cincinnati.

August Kautz—Civil War major general who commanded the cavalry of the Twenty-third Corps of the Union Army.

Reverend James Kemper—Born in Fauquier County, Virginia, the grandson of German immigrants from Siegen, he settled in Cincinnati with his family in 1791 and became the minister of the First Presbyterian Church of Cincinnati. His log house, now located at the Sharon Woods Village, is the oldest dwelling in what was the Miami Purchase and dates to circa 1793. Kemper Road is named in his honor.

Emil Klauprecht—Author of a novel on German-American life in Cincinnati, *Cincinnati, or the Mysteries of the West*, which has been called a major work in the history of German-American literature. Klauprecht also published the first history of the German-Americans in the Ohio Valley, *German Chronicle in the History of the Ohio Valley, and its Capital City, Cincinnati, in Particular.*

Bernard Kroger—Founding father of the grocery store business that bears his name.

Ernst Kunwald—Musical director of the Cincinnati Symphony Orchestra, who was interned during the First World War.

Ernst H. Huenefeld

Erich Kunzel—Popular musical director of the Cincinnati Pops Orchestra.

Wilhelm Lamprecht—Well-known artist whose work adorns many churches in the Greater Cincinnati area.

Leon Lippert—A student of Frank Duveneck's, whose paintings adorn many churches in the Greater Cincinnati area.

Tom Luken—A member of a family prominent in Cincinnati politics, who has served in Congress and as mayor of Cincinnati, as has his son, Charlie Luken. Tom Luken sponsored the proclamation in the House of Representatives, also submitted in the Senate, that established 6 October as national German-American Day in 1987.

John M. Meier—Founder of Meier's Winery.

Henry Moeller—A popular archbishop of Cincinnati for whom Moeller High School is named.

Christian Moerlein—One of the major pre-World War I brewers, whose name still appears on an area beer.

August Moor—Organized the second Cincinnati German regiment in the Civil War (the Twenty-eighth), and rose to the rank of brigadier general.

Wilhelm Nast—Founded the German Methodist Church in Cincinnati, which is located on Race Street across from Music Hall in Over-the-Rhine.

Gerhard Neumann—Engineer to vice president at General Electric for whom Neumann Way was named along interstate 75.

A. K. Nippert—A prominent German-American judge and community leader in the first half of the twentieth century, and member of a family prominent in Cincinnati history.

A. K. Nippert

Charlotte Pieper—Author of a work that has become a classic, *Wooden Shoe Hollow,* which describes life in the community located adjacent to Spring Grove Cemetery. Now available as a new edition, published by Little Miami Publishing Company and edited by the author of this guide.

Charlotte Pieper
(on left)

Heinrich A. Rattermann— Major German-American historian before World War I, whose company was the German Mutual Insurance Company, which was housed in the Germania Building at Twelfth and Walnut Street in Over-the-Rhine.

Charles Reemelin—First German-born person in Ohio elected to the Ohio State Legislature (1840s), where he helped revise the state constitution. Reemelin also campaigned for German instruction in the public schools, and was responsible for having the governor's message and other reports printed in German.

Heinrich A. Rattermann

Rev. Dr. Friedrich Reese—The first German Catholic priest in Cincinnati (1825).

Fritz Reiner—Well-known musical director of the Cincinnati Symphony Orchestra.

Heinrich Roedter—First major German-American newspaper editor, who edited the *Cincinnati Volksblatt*.

Max Rudolf—Well-known musical director of the Cincinnati Symphony Orchestra.

Eugene Ruehlmann—Former popular major of Cincinnati, who campaigned for the first baseball stadium on the riverfront.

Charles G. Schmidt—Founder of the Cincinnati Butcher Supply Company, one of the largest of its kind; his descendants donated several Schmidt rooms at the University of Cincinnati.

Johann Schmitt—Painted the murals at the "Church of the Steps" (Immaculata) in Mount Adams.

Herman Schneider—A dean of the College of Engineering at the University of Cincinnati who pioneered the idea of cooperative education.

Marge Schott—Automobile businesswoman and former owner of the Cincinnati Reds.

Al Schottelkotte—Television newsman known for his fact-packed live camera reports.

Jacob Seasongood (Suessengut)—Founder of a successful banking house, whose descendants were active in public affairs. He was considered a "self-made man" whose life was exemplary to other immigrants.

Jerry Springer—The son of German immigrants, he served as mayor of Cincinnati, and later became host of a national television talk show.

Reuben Springer—A Kentucky German-American who donated the funds for the construction of the Music Hall.

John B. Stallo—Prominent politician, philosopher and scholar. In 1860, he issued the call to Cincinnatians to support the cause of the Union, which led to the formation of the Ninth Ohio Regiment. Later, Stallo served as United States Minister to Italy.

Reuben Springer

Joseph Steger—Served for many years as president of the University of Cincinnati and transformed the campus into a showplace of signature architecture.

Albert von Stein—Promoter and builder of the Cincinnati waterworks, the first waterworks in the country that were worked by pumps.

Guy Stern—Head of the German Department at the University of Cincinnati and later Dean of Graduate Studies, who contributed to the study of German Exile Literature, as well as German-American Studies.

Adolph Strauch—Father of landscape gardening in America, who planned and designed Spring Grove Cemetery, Mount Storm Park, the Cincinnati Zoo, and influenced the planning of the parks in Cincinnati.

Frank van der Stucken—Well-known musical director of the Cincinnati Symphony Orchestra.

Gustaf Tafel—A Forty-eighter, who served in the Civil War, and later was elected mayor of Cincinnati.

John Henry Twachtman—Cincinnati-born German-American artist.

Charles F. Ullrich—German-born engraver who was commissioned by the Kraemer Art Company to create a 10 by 39-inch panoramic view of Cincinnati and Northern Kentucky that is considered the largest steel engraving in the world, and is entitled "Cincinnati in 1900."[2]

Gottfried Weitzel—Civil War major general who served in the Army of the Potomac under General Grant.

Michael Werk—Established the M. Werk and Company which specialized in candles and soap-making. The street, Werk Castle Lane, reminds us of his home, known as the Werk Castle, which was torn down in 1939. Werk had his arborist, Franz Josef Ernst, plant the trees along Werk Road. This street still bears his name, and honors this west side "soap king," who paved the way for many others such as Andrew Jergens who founded the Andrews Soap Company, later known as Andrew Jergens and Company.

Michael Werk

August von Willich—A Forty-eighter who organized and trained Cincinnati's all-German Ninth Ohio Regiment, as well as the Thirty-second Indiana German Regiment.

Isaac Meyer Wise—Father of Reform Judaism in America and an honorary member of the German Pioneer Society of Cincinnati.

Edwin H. Zeydel—Served for many years as Head of the German Department at the University of Cincinnati, and was internationally known for his numerous publications dealing with German literature.

David Ziegler—First mayor of Cincinnati, and a veteran of the American Revolution.

CHAPTER 4

GERMAN HERITAGE SITES IN OVER-THE-RHINE

T HERE IS A WEALTH OF SITES relating to the German heritage in Cincinnati, especially in the old German district known as Over-the-Rhine, which, although it may suffer the blight of modern urban decay and decline, nevertheless remains a treasure trove of noteworthy sites, several of which are highlighted as follows.[1]

The Over-the-Rhine District

The Over-the-Rhine district is bordered on the west and south by Central Parkway, on the east by Reading Road and Liberty, and by McMicken Avenue on the north. Among the many historic points of interest here are the following.

ST. JOHN'S PROTESTANT CHURCH/ DEUTSCHE PROTESTANTISCHE SANKT JOHANNES KIRCHE

Located on the northwest corner of Twelfth and Elm Streets. Cincinnati's first German-American congregation, formed in 1814, built this church in 1867. The congregation, now the Saint John's Unitarian Church, celebrated its 175th anniversary in 1989.

WASHINGTON PARK

Located between Race, Elm, Twelfth, and Fourteenth Streets. This park opened in 1861 and became a focal point for social, cultural, and political activities. The park contains a bandstand and statues of Friedrich Hecker (1811–1881) and Robert L. McCook.

St. John's Protestant Church

Early photograph of Washington Park with Music Hall in the background.

Hecker, a leader of the 1848 Revolution in Germany, came to Cincinnati in 1848, and founded the Turner Society in Cincinnati. At the outbreak of the Civil War, he joined the Union Army and rose to the rank of brigadier general. The inscription on the Hecker monument reads: "Mit Wort und That fuer Volksfreiheit im alten und neuen Vaterlande" (With Word and Deed for the Freedom of the People in the Old and New Fatherland). Colonel McCook commanded the all-German Ninth Ohio Regiment, formed by the Turner Society.

MUSIC HALL

Located at 1243 Elm Street. Formerly the site of a wooden hall (Saengerfest-Halle) where several German singing societies met, until the old hall was razed to make room for the new Music Hall, which opened in 1878. Today it is the home of the Cincinnati Symphony Orchestra.

SIXTH DISTRICT SCHOOL

Located on the corner of Elm Street. This was one of the more than forty German bilingual schools in Cincinnati before World War I. Among its principals was Dr. Heinrich H. Fick, later Superintendent of the German Department of the Public Schools. In 1935, his personal

Elm Street School in Sixth District

library was acquired by the University of Cincinnati and became the basis for the German-Americana Collection, established in 1974.

FINDLAY MARKET BUILDING

Located at 1800 Elm Street. This market building is named after James Findlay (1770–1835), an early Irish-American mayor of Cincinnati and United States congressman, who was popular with German-Americans because he opposed Prohibition. The present building has been in use since 1854, and is the only market building left in Cincinnati. Even today, many German-style products can be acquired here.

CHRISTIAN MOERLEIN BUILDING

Located on the east side of Elm and south of McMicken Streets. Christian Moerlein started brewing in the 1850s and his brewery became the largest in Cincinnati by 1891. It closed during Prohibition, and never reopened. The remaining buildings on Elm Street are the bottling plant, which was built around 1900, and the barrel house, which was erected in 1870.

The 1925 Opening Day celebration for the
Cincinnati Reds baseball team at Findlay Market.
For eighty-eight years, the Reds baseball season has begun with a parade commencing at Findlay Market. Stegner's Meat store, owned by Clarence Stegner, can be seen in the background. Photograph provided by Peggy Schmidt.

PHILIPPUS UNITED CHURCH OF CHRIST/
PHILIPPUS KIRCHE

Located on the northwest corner of Race and McMicken Avenue. This church, originally part of the German Reformed Church, was built in 1890, and German services were held here until the 1980s. Currently, the church is active in the local community. It houses an organ donated by Christian Moerlein.

SALEM CHURCH OF CHRIST
SALEM GERMAN EVANGELICAL REFORMED CHURCH/
DEUTSCHE EVANGELISCH REFORMIERTE SALEMS KIRCHE

Located on the southwest corner of Sycamore and Liberty Streets. This church was constructed in 1867 and services were held in German until the 1930s. The German name of the church is engraved over the front door on Sycamore Street.

SAINT PAUL CHURCH

Located on the southeast corner of Twelfth and Spring Streets. German Catholics constructed this church in 1849 and the roof and steeple were rebuilt after a fire in 1899. Note the German-made stained glass windows.

ALMS AND DOEPKE BUILDING

Located at 22 Central Parkway. William Alms, Frederick Alms, and William Doepke, all sons of German immigrants, opened a department store at this site in 1865 and erected the present building in 1878. The department store lasted until the 1950s and the building now houses governmental offices of Hamilton County.

GERMAN BAPTIST CHURCH/BAPTISTEN KIRCHE

Located on the southeast corner of Walnut and Corwine Streets. German Baptists built this church in 1866 and Cincinnati became a center of the German Baptists before World War I.

OLD SAINT MARY'S CHURCH/SAINT MARIEN KIRCHE

Located at 125 East Thirteenth Street. This Catholic church was erected by its German parishioners in 1841. Note the German inscription above the front door: "St. Marien Kirche, 1841." The interior was redecorated in 1890. Remarkable are the three oil paintings from Germany and the stained glass windows, of which one reads: "Maria, bitt für uns," or "Mary, pray for us." A German Mass is held Sundays at 11:00 A.M.

GERMAN MUTUAL INSURANCE COMPANY OF CINCINNATI/ DEUTSCHE GEGENSEITIGE VERSICHERUNGS-GESELLSCHAFT VON CINCINNATI

Located on the southwest corner of Walnut and Thirteenth Streets. This German-American insurance company was founded by Heinrich A. Rattermann on Vine Street in 1858, and had its offices here from 1870 until it moved to the Germania building in 1877, located one block to the south. The company's German name is still visible on the building.

Germania Building

Located on the southwest corner of Walnut and Twelfth Streets. The German Mutual Insurance Company constructed this building in 1877. Note the statue of Germania symbolizing the German spirit, which stands in a niche in the front of the building. During the First World War, the German inscription at the top of the building was covered up.

Photo shows the statue of Germania that appears in the niche in front of the Germania Building.

Kolping Society Building

Located at 1523 Republic Street. Built in 1870, this house was first used as a police station and later as a bath house. The German Kolping Society acquired the building in 1926, and owned it until 1958. The motto "Gott Segne das Ehrbare Handwerk," or "God Bless the Honorable Craft," is engraved over the front door.

Prince of Peace Lutheran Church (Trinity Church)/ Evangelisch-Lutherische Dreifaltigkeits-Gemeinde

Located at 1522 Race Street. This church was built by German Lutherans in 1871, and German services were held here until 1969 when the congregation, Concordia Lutheran Church, moved to its current location on Central Parkway, where German services are still held.

Saint Paul's German Evangelical Church/ Deutsche Evangelische Paulus Kirche

Located on the southwest corner of Fifteenth and Race Streets. Built in 1850, this church was founded by Northern Germans who split from Saint John's Protestant Church after disputes with the Southern German members of the congregation. The inscription above the front door reads: "Wahrheit, Tugend, Freiheit," or "Truth, Virtue, Freedom." The drugstore in the corner was opened after the church was built in order to pay off debts from the church's construction.

Germania Building

NAST TRINITY METHODIST CHURCH/
NAST METHODISTISCHE KIRCHE

Located at 1310 Race Street. This church is named after Wilhelm Nast, the German-born preacher and missionary who founded the world's first German Methodist church in Cincinnati in 1835. The congregation built its first church on this site in 1842, which was later replaced by the present church on this site in 1880. Note the German inscription over the front door: "Erste Bauerrichtet 1842—Neu Erbaut 1880," or; "First Built, 1842—Rebuilt 1880."

FIRST ENGLISH LUTHERAN CHURCH

Located on Race Street across from Washington Park. The English Lutheran Church differed from other Over-the-Rhine churches in that it was formed by German-Americans who wanted to have their church services in English, so that their children would learn the language, as they attended the bilingual schools and spoke mainly German in the district.

GRAMMER'S RESTAURANT

Located at 1440 Walnut Street. This restaurant was established by German-born Anton Grammer (1832–1911) in 1872. It soon flourished and became well known for its fine foods, beers, and liquors. The German Bakers Singing Society, the German Literary Club, the city fathers, and local politicians met here regularly. Note the glass windows in the front, which were imported from Germany in 1911.

Grammer's Restaurant, a well-known German restaurant in the Over-the-Rhine district. Photograph from the author's collection.

In 1887, Frank Grammer, Jr., (above) began working at the restaurant that his father, Anton, founded in 1872. He was born on Bremen Street (later changed to Republic Street in World War I) in the Over-the-Rhine district. Photograph from the author's collection.

Ich bin die Auferstehung und das Leben
I am the Resurrection and the Life

Religious monument created by Clement H. Barnhorn and located in the Mother of God Church Cemetery in Covington, Kentucky.

CHAPTER 5

GERMAN HERITAGE SITES IN COVINGTON

T hERE ARE MANY SITES in Covington relating to the German heritage, especially in the MainStrasse German Village.[1]

The MainStrasse German Village

Located on the west side of Covington, the MainStrasse German Village represents a relatively well preserved and maintained German district containing many shops, restaurants, saloons, specialty gift shops, etc. Points of interest here are as follows.

THE GOOSE GIRL FOUNTAIN

Located in the center of the village is this fountain, commissioned by the Northern Kentucky Convention and Visitors Bureau, and completed by the Greek company, Karkadoulias Bronze Art. The fountain is based on a German fairy tale by the famous Grimm brothers, "The Goose Girl."

Legend has it that the queen gave her daughter a magic handkerchief to protect her on her journey to be wed to a prince in a far away land. When stopping at a stream to water the horses, the princess dropped the handkerchief in the water, and an evil handmaiden, finding her powerless, took over the princess's horse and gown. When they arrived at the castle, the fake princess sent the real princess to a farmer saying she was a goose girl.

Each day she would herd geese and at the end of the day, the goose girl would unbraid her hair and cry. One day, the farmer heard her crying and found out the truth, whereupon he took her to the king and told the whole truth of what had happened. The prince and real princess were then married and lived happily the rest of their lives, and the fake princess was imprisoned. The fountain was dedicated in October 1980.

Goose Girl Fountain by Karkadoulias Bronze Art
Covington, Kentucky

THE GOEBEL PARK

Located on the west side of the Village, the park is a focal point, and is named in honor of William Goebel, a German-American elected governor of Kentucky in 1900. The park contains a major tourist attraction, a Glockenspiel, which was dedicated in 1979. It is known as the Carroll Chimes Bell Tower, as it is named in honor of then-Governor of Kentucky, Julian Carroll. The German Gothic Glockenspiel plays a forty-three-bell carillon hourly to present mini-concerts and the lively enactment of the German folklore of the tale "The Pied Piper of Hamelin."

Glockenspiel in Goebel Park
Covington, Kentucky

PERSHING/BREMEN STREET

Located south of the Goose Girl Fountain, just off of MainStrasse, is Pershing Street, which originally was Bremen Street. This was one of the streets and institutions whose name was changed during the First World War due to the anti-German hysteria of the time.

Sites Adjacent to MainStrasse Village

There are a number of sites of interest located adjacent to, or nearby, the German Village, including the following.

MUTTER GOTTES KIRCHE/MOTHER OF GOD CHURCH

Located at 119 West Sixth Street, this church was built by the German Catholics of Covington in 1870/71 with funds from the Leopoldine Mission Society of Vienna. Considered the most beautiful German-American church in the Greater Cincinnati area, it contains five murals by the German-American artist, Johann Schmitt, who trained Duveneck. The large stained-glass windows at the ends of the transept were imported from Munich in 1890. The one on the left depicts the Immaculate Conception and the one on the right depicts the Assumption. The art windows along the sides of the church, for the most part, represent Old Testament promises in the lower panels and their New Testament fulfillment in the upper panels.

The decorative frescoes by Wenceslaus Thien, another German-American artist, are noted for their design and color harmony. The artistry of Krienhagen above the windows expresses symbolism from the Litany of Loretto. The large crucifix behind the main altar was the work of the Covington German sculptor, Ferdinand Muer. It was blessed in 1871, and originally installed at the communion rail. The

Stations of the Cross were done by Paul Deschwanden in 1872. The tower clocks were installed in 1875 and are 110 feet from the floor, and 8 feet in diameter. The organ, installed in 1876, was made by A. Koehnken and Grimm, and is considered one of the finest in the west. The brothers/pastors, William and Henry Tappert, are buried at the altar of our Lady of Perpetual Help at the right rear of the church. Oil paintings of them hang in the choir loft. The picture of our Lady of Perpetual Help at the altar was received by Father William Tappert from Pope Leo XIII in private audience, 22 August 1882. The wooden carved altars are the work of Henry and Frederick Schroeder and the communion table and pulpit are the work of Donnenfelser.

The church was consecrated in 1903. The main marble altar was constructed in anticipation of the consecration and a mosaic English cut tile floor was laid around it. The twelve marble crosses along the sides of the church were placed for the ceremony in conformance with the requirements of the consecration. A lighted candle placed over each at the beginning of the service represents the twelve apostles—the "light of the world."

The German Mettlach tile main and side aisles were laid in 1921, the same year in which the Carrara angels with holy water bowls in the back of the church were given to the parish. The marble baptistry at the left rear of the church was added in 1929. The stone statues of Saints Peter and Paul and the two mythological lions in front of the church were completed at the Mayer Royal Art Institute in Munich.

GRACE UNITED CHURCH OF CHRIST

Located at Lockwood and Willard Street, the building of this German Reformed Church was dedicated in 1863, but during the First World War changed its name to the Grace Reformed Church due to the anti-German hysteria of the time. It is now part of the United Church of Christ. Note the historic marker in the front of the church.

THE TURNER HALL

Located at 447 Pike Street, this hall was built in 1877 by the Covington Turners, the oldest German-American society in Covington, which was founded in 1855.

Turner Hall

THE BAVARIAN BREWING COMPANY

Located just south of the MainStrasse village, the Bavarian Brewing Company began as the Deglow Brewing Company in 1866. It became the Bavarian Brewing Company in 1870, and under the direction of William Riedlin, became a major brewery. By 1896, it produced thirty-two thousand barrels of beer annually. In 1934, the brewery reopened after Prohibition, and continued operation into the 1960s. In 1996 it reopened after extensive renovation as a brewpub, restaurant, and party store. Its location alongside Interstate 75 contributes effectively in presenting the German heritage of Covington to passers-by.

The Riverfront Area

Among the sites in this area, the most notable are as follows.

THE JOHN A. ROEBLING SUSPENSION BRIDGE

Completed in 1867, the bridge is a veritable symbol of the entire Greater Cincinnati area, and it connects Covington and Cincinnati. It is considered Roebling's model for his world-famous Brooklyn Bridge, which was completed after this bridge. Widely viewed as an architectural and historic landmark, it is also considered symbolic of the area—a bridge built by a German immigrant, Johann August Roebling. The bridge was completed on New Year's Day 1867. Its cost is estimated at $1.8 million to build and measures 1,057 feet between the 230-foot-high towers, and 1,619 feet between the shore anchors.

The bridge was placed on the National Register of Historic Places in 1975, and illuminated with lights in 1984 in honor of Julia Langsam, president of the Covington and Cincinnati Bridge Company and wife of Dr. Walter Langsam, president of the University of Cincinnati, as well as a well-known German-American historian.

THE ROEBLING MONUMENT

Located at the foot of the bridge, at its southeast corner, is a statue depicting Roebling, which bears the following inscription: "From an Immigrant to an Immigrant. John A. Roebling and to all Immigrants who have helped build Greater Cincinnati, from Matth. Toebben and his family." Note that the funds for the monument came from a well-known German-American in the construction industry in northern Kentucky, Matth. Toebben.

THE AMOS SHINKLE TOWNHOUSE

Located at 210 Garrard Street, this townhouse belonged to the Covington German, Amos Shinkle (1811–92), who was a leading businessman in the area, the major promoter of the Roebling Suspension Bridge, and president of the Covington and Cincinnati Bridge Co. The home, a two-story brick townhouse, was built in 1854 and described by a columnist as follows: "Mr. Shinkle is one of our most enterprising businessmen, and in arranging for this building seems to have been actuated by a determination to combine elegance and convenience, regardless of cost."

SHINKLE'S ROW

Shinkle built a series of seven townhouses located at 230–242 East Second Street. This row of Renaissance Revival townhouses was his largest residential building project, and was restored in the mid-1970s.

The Ernst Home

Located at 401 Garrard Street, this home belonged to the Pennsylvania German banker, William Ernst (1813–95), who served as president of the Northern Bank of Kentucky, located at East Third Street and Scott Boulevard. His son, John P. Ernst, also served as president of the bank but resigned to become president of the family's other bank, the German National Bank, located on Madison Avenue.

The Wolff Printing Company

Located at the corner of Court and Greenup Streets, this building housed the office of one of the major German-American printing companies in the Greater Cincinnati area, which printed materials in German and English for the greater part of the twentieth century.

Sites South of the Riverfront

Directly south of the riverfront area are the following historic sites.

The Duveneck House

Located at 1226 Greenup Street, this was the home of Frank Duveneck (1848–1919), considered the premier German-American artist of the area. After having been apprenticed to Covington's Institute of Catholic Art, he went to Munich in 1869 where he studied at the Royal Academy of Fine Arts. After living in various places in Europe and America, Duveneck accepted a permanent appointment in 1900 at the Art Academy of Cincinnati. It was said that he was the greatest painter of his generation, and his influence was extensive due to his many students.

The Cathedral Basilica

Located on Madison Avenue between Eleventh and Twelfth Streets, this church was modeled after Notre Dame, and contains the works of German and German-American artists. Mayer and Company of Munich produced the stained-glass windows on the lower and clerestory levels. Four murals for the chapel and a triptych on the east wall were donated by Frank Duveneck. The well-known German-American sculptor, Clement Barnhorn, produced the statue of the Madonna and the carving of the Assumption of Mary above the front door of the cathedral.

The South Side of Covington

Especially noteworthy on the south side of Covington is the Mother of God Church Cemetery, located on Madison Pike. The cemetery contains numerous beautiful monuments, many of them carved with German inscriptions, as well as the following noteworthy sites.

ICH BIN DIE AUFERSTEHUNG UND DAS LEBEN/ I AM THE RESURRECTION AND THE LIFE

This magnificent religious monument was created by the German-American sculptor, Clement H. Barnhorn, and was dedicated in May 1915.

THE KUEHR MONUMENT

Located near Barnhorn's statue is the final resting place of Father Kuehr, the founding father of the Mutter Gottes Kirche. Also nearby are the resting places of other members of the clergy.

THE DUVENECK MONUMENT

A beautiful monument marks the grave of the German-American artist, Frank Duveneck, and other members of his family.

The Duveneck Monument

Hauck House Museum
Cincinnati, Ohio

CHAPTER 6

MUSEUMS AND LIBRARIES

Museums

T HERE ARE SEVERAL MUSEUMS in the Greater Cincinnati area that are of particular interest with regard to the German heritage of the region.[1]

HAUCK HOUSE MUSEUM

Located at 812 Dayton Street in the West End, this museum is in the home of the prominent German-American brewer, John Hauck. Telephone: 513-561-8842.

GERMAN HERITAGE MUSEUM

Located at West Fork Park, 4764 West Fork Road, the museum contains exhibits on the German heritage of the region, and provides information on the German-American community of the area. Telephone: 513-598-9989.

CINCINNATI ART MUSEUM

Located in Eden Park, 953 Eden Park Drive, the museum includes works of art by area German-American artists. Telephone: 513-721-5204.

WALDSCHMIDT HOUSE

Located at 7509 Glendale-Milford Road, this was the home of one of the early German settlers, Christian Waldschmidt and family. Telephone: 513-576-6327

The Waldschmidt House

TAFT MUSEUM OF ART

Located at 316 Pike Street, the museum was built around 1820, and was originally the home of Martin Baum. According to the museum's Web site it is "the oldest domestic wooden structure in situ locally and is considered one of the finest examples of Federal architecture in the Palladian style in the country." Among others, the house later belonged to Nicholas Longworth, David Sinton, and then the Taft family, and opened as the Taft Museum in 1932. Telephone: 513-241-0343.

CINCINNATI HISTORY MUSEUM AND HISTORICAL SOCIETY

Located at Union Terminal, 1301 Western Avenue, the center has exhibits on the history of Cincinnati. Telephone: 513-287-7000.

THE BEHRINGER-CRAWFORD MUSEUM

Located west of Covington's MainStrasse German Village in Devou Park, the museum promoted local history and heritage through its exhibits and programs, and also contains a library focusing on the region. Telephone: 859-491-4003.

Taft Museum. Former home of Martin Baum. Photo by Tony Walsh.
Printed with permission from the Taft Museum.

THE BENNINGHOFEN HOUSE

The home of a former prominent German-American businessman serves as the home of the Butler County Historical Society in nearby Hamilton, Ohio, which is located north of Cincinnati. The Benninghofen House, 327 North Second Street, is located in Hamilton's German Village Historic District. Telephone: 513-896-9930.

Libraries

There are many libraries in the region, but the following are of special interest with regard to the German heritage.

CINCINNATI HISTORICAL SOCIETY LIBRARY

Located at the Cincinnati Museum Center, 1301 Western Avenue, the Historical Society contains a wealth of information on the history of the area. Telephone: 513-287-7000. Web site: <http://www.cincymuseum.org>.

The Benninghofen House

German-Americana Collection

Located in the Archives and Rare Books Department, Blegen Library University of Cincinnati, the collection is one of the major collections of its kind. Telephone: 513-556-1955. Web site: <http://www.archives.uc.edu/german>.

Kenton County Public Library

Location in Covington, 502 Scott Street, the library maintains an excellent local history collection. Telephone: 859-491-7610. Web site: <http://www.kenton.lib.kyus>.

Public Library of Cincinnati and Hamilton County

Located in downtown Cincinnati, 800 Vine Street, the Public Library has one of the major genealogical collections in the United States. Telephone: 513-369-6905. Web site: <http://www.plch.lib.oh.us>.

CHAPTER 7

GERMAN HALLS

German-American Citizens League

THE GERMAN-AMERICAN CITIZENS LEAGUE OF GREATER CIN-CINNATI (GACL), founded in 1895, serves as the umbrella organization of German-American societies in the region, maintains the German Heritage Museum in Cincinnati, and sponsors the annual German Day in June, as well as the German-American Heritage Month in October. Although most organizations affiliated with the GACL are in the Greater Cincinnati area, there are now several in the tristate region of Ohio, Kentucky, and Indiana.

Information on the organizations affiliated with the GACL can be found at its Web site (www.gacl.org) and also in the GACL newspaper, *The German-American Chronicle of the Ohio Valley.* The Web site and the newspaper provide information on the various organizations in the region, their histories, activities, and events.[1]

The GACL Web site provides the following history of the league, its functions, and activities:

> In 1883, the German-American Bicentennial of the founding of Germantown, Pennsylvania, the first all-German settlement in America, was celebrated on the 6th of October in Cincinnati. Instrumental in organizing this celebration was the Pionier-Verein (German Pioneer Society), and especially its members Heinrich A. Rattermann and Dr. H.H. Fick. The 1883 Bicentennial was called Pastorius Day in honor of Germantown's founder, Franz Daniel Pastorius.

> Thereafter, Pastorius Day came to be known simply as Deutscher Tag, or German Day, and was held sporadically until the celebration in 1895 at the Cincinnati Zoo attracted 12,000 people. Part of the entertainment that day was provided by the newly formed Cincinnati Symphony Orchestra. As a result of the tremendous success of the

event, it was decided that the celebration would be held annually. To facilitate this, an organization called the German Day Society (Deutsche Tag-Gesellschaft) was created. Additional goals were also designated by the newly formed group, primarily directed at combating the then prevalent [P]rohibition movement and the anti-bilingual movement in schools. Both movements were defeated in Cincinnati thanks to the work of the organization.

The German Day Society changed its name to the German-American Alliance when it became an affiliate of the National German-American Alliance in 1906. Due to the anti-German hysteria of World War I, the Alliance was forced to change its name again, just as street names, businesses, etc. were also being changed. It became the American Citizens League (Amerikanische Buerger-Liga) until after World War II, when, acknowledging its roots, it became the German-American Citizens League (Deutsch-Amerikanische Buerger-Liga).

Judge John Schwaab, who also served on the Cincinnati Board of Education, served as President of the Buerger-Liga for many years. Other prominent individuals involved with the League were Judge A. K. Nippert and Judge August Bode. The League's meeting place for many years was at the Turner Hall, located at 12th and Walnut Streets in the Over-the-Rhine district and later at the Steuben Hall on Rohs Street. Currently the League meets at the Greene Lodge in Green Township.

Since 1895, the League has served as the central German-American umbrella association in the area, and continues to actively support and promote the civic, social, and cultural interests of the German-American community. The League's membership is comprised of the delegates from the many German-American organizations in the greater Cincinnati area. The general purpose of the League is to coordinate, represent, and promote German-American interests and culture.

Of the various organizations in the Greater Cincinnati area, the following maintain their own clubhouses, or German houses. Some of these also have quite extensive grounds for sports activities, as well as festivities.

Cincinnati Central Turners

Located at 200 Pinney Lane, Cincinnati, Ohio, 45231. Founded in

1848, the Turners were the first Turnverein in the United States, and subscribed to the Turner philosophy of a "sound body and a sound mind," which they practiced, according to the GACL Web site,

at the corner of 12th and Vine in the open air, and shortly after in a small building on Walnut Street, where Turner Hall was built. By 1850, the Turner School had 380 boys and 90 girls enrolled in gymnastic classes. This same year saw the Society become incorporated at the German Turner Society of Cincinnati. The following year, they joined the newly founded North American Turner Association (Turnerbund).

In 1851, construction was completed on a building on Walnut Street. By 1859, the building was too small and the well-known Turner Hall was built. In 1852, the national Turner Fest was held in Cincinnati. A year later, a Schuetzen Company was formed, as well as a band. In 1854, the town of New Ulm, Minnesota was founded by the Cincinnati Turner Colonization Society, led by Wilhelm Pfaender, with the goal of establishing a German-American town on the frontier. During the Civil War, the Turners comprised the entire 9th Ohio voluntary Infantry Regiment.

In the 19th century, the Turners played an important role in Cincinnati by introducing physical education into the public schools (1892), as well as supporting the instruction of the German language in schools. Before World War I, Turner Hall was the home of the German Theater, and was the central meeting place for the German-American societies of Cincinnati. The Turners also supported a German library and were known for the many cultural programs they sponsored.

In the 1950s, the Turners moved out of the Turner Hall on Walnut St. to their current location on Pinney Lane in Springfield Township. The old Turner Hall was torn down in 1972.

In 1998, the Cincinnati Central Turners celebrated their 150th anniversary. The Turners are the oldest German-American society in Cincinnati and the oldest Turner Society in America.

COVINGTON TURNERS

Located at 447 Pike Street, Covington, Kentucky 41011. Founded in 1855, the Covington Turners agreed to the following points at their founding: opposition to Prohibition, the Know-Nothing Party, and the institution of slavery. According to the Web site of the Kenton County Library:

> In 1857, the Covington Turners acquired a home on Pike Street. These new facilities included an area for exercise, a saloon and meeting rooms. The outbreak of the Civil War, however, nearly dissolved the society. Many members joined the Union Army and marched off to war. By 1864, only seven Turners remained in the organization. Following the war, members again increased. In 1870, a new building was acquired for the society at the corner of Pike and Ninth Streets.
>
> During these years, the society sponsored singing events, gymnastic training, political debates, rifle shooting contests and various contests. A junior section was also established to ensure that young Germans were being properly trained. In 1877, the society began planning for the construction of a permanent hall. On May 10, the cornerstone of the new building was officially set into place. The new hall was dedicated on October 1.
>
> In the early years of the society, the wives and mothers of the members assisted the men at society activities. In 1899, the first official Women's Auxiliary was established...Members of the Women's Auxiliary were instrumental in the...golden jubilee of the Covington Turner Society which was celebrated in 1905. At that time, membership stood at 150.
>
> The use of the German language was discontinued at the Turner meetings in 1915. The 1950s witnessed great change for the Turners. Membership dropped as Covington residents began moving to the suburbs. On a more progressive note, women were accepted as full members in 1950. This decision increased membership and provided a greater stability within the organization. In 1955, the 100th anniversary of the Covington Turners was celebrated with appropriate festivities.
>
> During the 1960s and 1970s, the Turners sponsored both basketball and baseball teams for youth. In 1967, a youth club was established. These efforts brought new life to the society.

DONAUSCHWABEN SOCIETY

Located at 4290 Dry Ridge Road, Cincinnati, Ohio 45252. The Donauschwaben maintain their own clubhouse and grounds for sports activities, and are described at the GACL Web site as follows:

> The Donauschwaben people are people of German heritage. Their ancestors left Germany in the eighteenth century and settled in southeastern Europe along the Danube River, in what is today part of Yugoslavia, Hungary, and Romania. There they converted the swamplands of the Danube Basin into fertile farmland. While living in their new homeland, they kept their German language, customs and traditions alive.
>
> During and after World War II, many Donauschwaben perished in Yugoslavian and Russian concentration camps. All were dispossessed; many were uprooted and dispersed. Today, you can find Donauschwaben all over the globe.
>
> The Donauschwaben Society of Cincinnati was founded in 1954. While being solid and proud citizens of the United States, Donauschwaben still strive to nurture the customs and traditions of their ancestors and to pass them on to the younger generation by their example.
>
> The Society sponsors various activities for all ages, including singing, dancing, bands, sports, and senior groups. At the current home in Colerain Township, they celebrate such traditional events as the Strauss Ball, Donauschwaben Day, Oktoberfest and Kirchweih, as well as many other festivities in the old world tradition.
>
> The Cincinnati Donauschwaben Society is open to all people who respect and appreciate the values and cultural activities of the Donauschwaben.

GERMANIA SOCIETY

Located at 3529 West Kemper Road, Cincinnati, Ohio 45251. The Germania Society maintains its own clubhouse and grounds for festivities, and is described by the GACL Web site as follows:

> The Germania Society was founded in 1964 as a society of German heritage. The purpose of the Germania Society is to perpetuate the German culture and to establish true traditional events of German

folklore.

The idea for the Society was conceived in 1960 by a few forward thinking immigrants who resolved that a new society was needed in Cincinnati, and one which would include people from all Germanic areas, but refrain from politics and religion. The name Germania was chosen in 1963, and by the end of that year, meetings were held to ratify a constitution. The Germania Society was incorporated on May 16, 1964.

The Germania Society contributed to the already rich list of German-American events in Cincinnati. A radio program called *Over-the-Rhine Showcase* was started in 1963 by founding board member Hermann Albers, and was followed by Over-the-Rhine Day at LeSourdsville Lake in 1964. Oktoberfest dances were the forerunners of Cincinnati's Original Oktoberfest, begun by Germania in 1971. Charter flights to Germany were organized, and entertainers...were brought to Cincinnati from Germany. Original involvement in Maifest and the International Folk Festival is credited to President Fred Mause and Helmut Maurer.

Under the direction of Germania founding board member, Dr. Wilhelm Kraehling, a German school program was introduced, now called the Tri-State German-American School. The *Cincinnati Kurier* was newly published by Marie Lammers Engel, and Germania's first article appeared on December 18, 1964, written by founding board member, Ernst Schwab, who wrote many more articles in an effort to promote Germania, as well as to establish a Rhineland style Karneval organization within the Society. In 1967, President Fritz Prochnow and his wife, LaNelle, became the first princely couple. The Elfferrat (council of eleven jesters) has chosen a prince every year since 1968. In 1977, the Germania Society completed their Klubhaus, located on West Kemper Road in Springfield Township.The outdoor pavillion was built in 1985 and is the site of Cincinnati's Original Oktoberfest, held each year in August.

The Germania Society has given the people of Cincinnati many years of enjoyment through its many cultural events. All people of German birth, Germanic people, and those of German ancestry are eligible for membership.

KOLPING SOCIETY

Located at 10235 Mill Road, Cincinnati, Ohio 45231. The Kolping Society maintains its own clubhouse and grounds, and is described at the GACL Web site as follows:

Blessed Father Adolph Kolping founded the Kolping Society in 1849 in Elberfeld, Germany as a journeyman's society or Gesellenverein. At that time, journeymen from all trades were expected to work with master craftsmen in different towns in order to get a variety of experiences before settling in one place. Their quarters were almost always substandard. Father Kolping established houses, somewhat on the order of the YMCA facilities, that provided affordable accommodations in a Christian atmosphere. His motto was, and is today: 'Good families make a good nation.' The Kolping Society has always supported mankind by fostering the spirituality of the individual, integrity of the family, devotion to one's vocation and loyalty to one's country.

In 1924, the seeds to the present Cincinnati Kolping Center and its sports complex were planted by the thirteen members who founded the original Cincinnati Kolping branch on Republic Street in the Over-the-Rhine area. In the 1950s, the Kolping Society on Winton Road was developed. The Cincinnati Kolping Society has grown to over 1000 members and is now one of the largest Kolping families in the world.

The search for a larger facility led to the purchase of fifty-seven acres from St. Francis Seminary in 1980. The Cincinnati Kolping Society now owns fifty-two acres, a third of which is wooded…This facility, known as Kolping Park, houses four soccer fields, three lighted baseball/softball diamonds, volleyball courts, a maintenance and recreation building and a children's play area. The Society has a large clubhouse/hall facility called the Kolping Center. Behind the Kolping Center is an outdoor pavillion and beer garden adjoining the woods.

The Kolping Society consists of many subgroups, including the Kolping Sports Club, Schuetzen Club, Pigeon Club, Teen Club, Young Adults, Senior Citizens, Tuesday Workers, Kolping Saengerchor, King's Court, Gold Club, and Kolping Band. Various activities ares sponsored throughout the year by these groups, affording wholesome recreation, athletic events, educational, cultural, musical and social opportunities for members as well as the general community.

LIBERTY HOME GERMAN SOCIETY

Located at 2361 Hamilton-Cleves Road, Hamilton, Ohio 45013. With its own clubhouse and grounds, this society is described at the GACL Web site as follows:

The Liberty Home German Society can possibly trace its origins to an organization known as the Allgemeiner Deutscher Unterstuetzungs Verein, or the universal German Assistance Club. A newspaper article, appearing on June 9, 1903, stated that the ADUV's 'seventy year old picnic will take place at Ohlinger's on July 4, 1903.' This would indicate that the ADUV could have been an active organization as early as 1837. In 1903, the German Federation of Hamilton was formed, consisting of seven German-American organizations, representing 900 members. The minutes of the first meeting indicate representation from the AADUV. The purpose of the Federation was to unite all Germans and to protect their interests in their adopted country.

As World War I loomed, the German Federation of Hamilton began to lose members. Many of those who had claimed alliance with the German Federation slowly transferred their interests to the Deutscher Hausverein, or Liberty Home German Society.

As America entered World War I, it became unpopular to claim membership in any organization that retained German customs and lifestyles. On May 5, 1918, it was decided to change the name of the organization to Liberty Home Society. On July 10, 1919, incorporation papers were drawn and Liberty Home became the legal name of the association, which it retains to this date.

The period between the wars witnessed the Liberty Home Society participating in numerous public, patriotic, community and fraternal events. The severe immigration policies in place between 1918 and 1945 had an effect on membership. Not until the 1940s and 1950s did the German-speaking membership again begin to increase.

The Liberty Home Society still retains many of its German related, folksy events, where both young and old members can enjoy their culture.

The Liberty Home Society has given much to Hamilton County and

Butler County and still strives to retain, use and preserve German—
the real binding force for its existence.

SCHLARAFFIA SOCIETY

Located at 2357 Rohs Street, Cincinnati, Ohio 45219. This society has
its clubhouse, located near the University of Cincinnati, and is
described at the GACL Web site as being

> in the strict sense, a fraternity. Its clubs are spread all over the world
> and can be found on each continent. Artists and academicians in Prag
> (Prague), which was considered at the time the Mekka (Mecca) of
> German culture, founded the Schlaraffia Society in 1859. Its aim was
> to offset the chauvinistic and egoistic behavior of the nobility, and to
> create a hideout for men from the exertions and worries of the
> profane life. The Society's maxims consist of fostering art, humor,
> and friendship.

> An actor by the name of Victor Mueller-Fabricius founded the club in
> Cincinnati in 1893. Almost the whole Symphony Orchestra of
> Cincinnati joined the society at that time. The name of the Cincinnati
> settlement is Schlaraffia Cincinnatia. The official language used
> during meetings and correspondence is German.

> Many customs and some semantics of medieval times are used at the
> sessions, since Schlaraffia maintains its relationship to civic societies
> of the Medieval Age.

> During the meetings that occur weekly during the winter months and
> less often during the summer months, attendees listen to lectures
> prepared by speakers on such topics as problems of technique, art
> and literature. The lectures are followed by discussions where much
> wit and humor are usually exchanged.

> The place of Schlaraffia assemblies is called Burg. In Cincinnati, the
> Burg is the former Steuben House on Rohs Street in Clifton.

> The Society venerates the owl, called Uhu in German, as the emblem
> of wisdom. The owl was honored at the times of the Antike (Greek
> and Roman antiquity) as the representative of prudence and wisdom.
> Of the three goals of Schlaraffia, the most important one is the
> sincere friendship that glues the membership together and obligates
> each Schlaraffe to provide mutual aid and assistance according to his
> potential.

.

CHAPTER 8

LOCAL GERMAN RESOURCES

T HERE ARE MANY SITES OF INTEREST to explore in the area, and visitors are especially referred to chapters 4–7, which provide information on historic sites, as well as museums, libraries, and German halls. However, visitors might also want to obtain information about the area in advance of a visit or, once here, might want to find information, for example, on where German restaurants are located. This chapter, therefore, provides information not only about restaurants, but also about German church services, German radio programs, and other points of interest relating to the German heritage of the area. I hope it serves as a handy reference guide to finding your way around German Cincinnati.

GENERAL INFORMATION

General information for travelers and visitors can be obtained through the following visitors' centers:

Cincinnati USA & Visitors Bureau
525 Vine Street, Suite 1500
Cincinnati, Ohio 45202
Tel.: 513-621-2142
www.cincyusa.com

———

Northern Cincinnati Convention & Visitors Bureau
11641 Chester Road, Suite B
Cincinnati, Ohio 45246
Tel.: 888-552-4629
www.cincynorth.com

Northern Kentucky Convention & Visitors Bureau
One West River Center Blvd.
Covington, Kentucky 41011
Tel.: 859-261-1500
www.staynky.com

GERMAN-AMERICAN INFORMATION

General information about German festivals, functions, and activities sponsored by the German-American societies of the region can be found at the Web site of the German-American Citizens League (GACL), the umbrella organization of area organizations. Altogether, twenty-five German-American societies are affiliated with the GACL, which was founded in 1895. Among the festivals sponsored in the area are: German Day (first weekend in June), Schuetzenfest (mid-July), Oktoberfest (various festivals from late August through October), German-American Heritage Month (October), Christkindlmarkt (weekend before Thanksgiving), Saengerfest (December and May), and St. Nikolaus Day (first Sunday of December). For further information about these and other events, as well as the various German-American societies, see:

German-American Citizens League
www.gacl.org.

GERMAN-AMERICAN NEWSLETTER

The GACL also publishes a quarterly newsletter, *German-American News/Deutsch-Amerikanische Nachrichten*, which contains news, items of interest, and a calendar of events for the region. For further information, contact:

Marge Poole, Editor
German-American News
Deutsch-Amerikanische Nachrichten
one2print@aol.com

GERMAN-AMERICAN NEWSPAPER

The local German-language newspaper, *Der Cincinnati Kurier*, was acquired and absorbed by *Amerika-Woche*, which is now

Marge Poole, Editor
German-American News

published in Freeport, New York, but still carries news from the Greater Cincinnati area, as well as German-American communities nationwide. For further information, contact:

Amerika-Woche
100 S. Ocean Ave., Suite 1U
Freeport, New York 11520
Tel.: 516-771-3181
info@amerikawoche.com
www.amerikawoche.com

GERMAN-AMERICAN RADIO PROGRAMS

Several German-American radio programs in the area provide German music, as well as news about German-American events in the area. Tune in the following programs as follows:

Over-the-Rhine Showcase
Sundays: 1:00–6:00 p.m.
WOBO 88.7 FM
Host: Heinz Probst
Tel.: 513-271-0586

International Program
Tuesdays: Noon–3:00 p.m.
WOBO 88.7 FM
Host: Heinz Probst
Tel.: 513-271-0586

German Tunes of the Queen City
Wednesdays: 5:00–8:00 p.m.
WAIF 88.3 FM
Hosts: Hans Kroschke and Gebhard Erler
Tel.: 513-749-1444

Melodies of German & Austria Program
Saturdays: 10:00 a.m.–1:00 p.m.

WORP 89.5 FM
Hosts: Maritta Hall and Dieter Waldowski
Tel.: 937-865-5900

Another radio program of interest is *Mid-Morning with Wolf* hosted by Wolfgang Eschenlohr. His weekly program broadcasts big band music, as well as announcements on German-American festivities. Tune in the program as follows:

Mid-Morning with Wolf
Tuesdays 10:00–11:00 a.m.
WMKV 89.3 FM
Host: Wolfgang Eschenlohr
Tel.: 513-729-8330

If you are interested in classical music, the station to tune in to is WGUC–FM. Although it does not broadcast German-American programs, it does provide classical music, which includes many composers from the German-speaking countries, such as Beethoven, Bach, Mozart, etc. Tune in the station as follows:

Cincinnati's Classical Public Radio
WGUC 90.9 FM
Tel.: 513-241-8282

GERMAN-AMERICAN BANDS

German-American bands greatly contribute to the colorful and lively German-American musical scene in the Greater Cincinnati area. Several maintain websites that provide further information as to their programs and recordings.

Alpen Echos
www.alpenechos.com/

———

Cincinnati Schnapps Band
www.schnappsband.com

———

Nick Gulacsy
www.delphinius-management.com/photos.html

Co-host Gebhard Erler, WAIF 88.3 FM, also entertains at the Hofbräuhaus in Newport, Kentucky, on Thursdays from 3:00 to 6:00 p.m.

Postcard advertising the Alpen Echos Band.
Courtesy of the Alpen Echoes

———

Franz Klaber Orchestra
klaberheads.com/index.html

———

Pros't Band
www.prostband.com/

———

Pete Wagner Band
www.petewagnerband.com/

Other groups performing in the region include the Gebhard Erler Duo, the Jack Frost Accordion Band, and the Polka Dots. German-American bands perform widely at festivities and events throughout the region, and several of them also perform nationally as well.

GERMAN TELEVISION

German television is available via cable throughout the tri-state region, and is offered by different services. Check with your local cable television provider to see what cable channel offers German programming.

GERMAN CHURCH SERVICES

German church services are offered on a regular basis by the following churches:

Concordia Lutheran Church
1133 Clifton Hills Avenue
Cincinnati, Ohio
Services: Second Sunday of the month
Time: 9:00 a.m.
Tel.: 513-861-9552
www.concordia-cincy.org/

Old St. Mary's Church
123 East Thirteenth Street
Cincinnati, Ohio
Services: Sundays
Time: 11:00 a.m.
Tel.: 513-721-2988
www.oldstmarys.org/

GERMAN GIFTS

German gift items can be found at various shops throughout the area, but the following two in downtown Cincinnati and Covington are fairly convenient:

Linden Noll Gift Haus
506 West Sixth Street
Covington, Kentucky
Tel.: 859-581-7633

———

Saxony Imports
542 Race Street
Cincinnati, Ohio
Tel.: 513-621-7800
www.saxonyimports.com/

A fine selection of German gifts is also available at the Oktoberfest and the Christkindlmarkt sponsored by the Germania Society. The society maintains a gift booth at the Downtown Oktoberfest as well. Check the Web site of the Germania Society for the dates of its events.

Germania Society
www.germaniasociety.com/

RESTAURANTS AND CAFES

A variety of restaurants and cafes offer German cuisine, but it is wise to call them to check on their hours, which may vary by the season. Also, please note that many other restaurants and cafes in the area offer German-style food, such as goetta with breakfast, as this is an integral part of local cuisine. The following restaurants specialize in German food:

Black Forest Restaurant
8675 Cincinnati-Columbus Road
West Chester, Ohio
Tel.: 513-777-7600
www.theblackforest.com/

———

Brotzeit Deli
30 East Mulberry Street
Lebanon, Ohio 45036
Tel.: 513-282-6500

Brau Haus
22170 Water Street
Oldenburg, Indiana
Tel.: 812-934-4840
www.oldenburgbrauhaus.com/

German Cuisine
6517 Dixie Highway
Florence, Kentucky
Tel.: 859-746-1200

Germantowne Pizza Haus
West Twenty-sixth & Madison Avenue
Covington, Kentucky
Tel.: 859-431-0037

Hofbräuhaus Newport
Third & Saratoga at the Levee
Newport, Kentucky
Tel.: 859-491-7200
www.hofbrauhausnewport.com/

Iron Skillet
6900 Valley Avenue
Cincinnati, Ohio
Tel.: 513-561-6776

Kreimer's Bier Haus
6052 Ohio 128
Miamitown, Ohio
Tel.: 513-353-2168

Lenhardt's Restaurant
151 W. McMillan Avenue
Cincinnati, Ohio
Tel.: 513-281-3600
www.christysandlenhardts.com/history.htm

————

Mecklenburg Gardens
301 East University Avenue
Cincinnati, Ohio
Tel.: 513-221-5353
www.mecklenburgs.net/index.htm

————

Ron's Roost
3853 Race Road
Cincinnati, Ohio
Tel.: 513-574-0222

————

Sherman House
Batesville, Indiana
Tel.: 800-445-4939
www.sherman-house.com/

————

Steinkeller
15 East High Street
Oxford, Ohio
Tel.: 513-524-2437

————

Strasse Haus
630 Main Street
Covington, Kentucky
Tel.: 859-261-1199

————

Tom Harten standing at the entrance to Mecklenburg Gardens.

Wertheim's Restaurant
514 West Sixth Street
Covington, Kentucky
Tel.: 859-261-1233

———

Wiener Haus
2900 Dixie Highway
Crestview Hills, Kentucky
Tel.: 859-341-3240

MARKETS

German food can be found throughout the area at markets and grocery stores, such as the many Kroger grocery stores. Several good markets that are sure to carry German food items include the following:

Avril & Bleh Meat Market
33 East Court Street
Cincinnati, Ohio
Tel.: 513-241-2433

Findlay Market
1801 Race Street
Over-the-Rhine District
Cincinnati, Ohio
Tel.: 513-665-4839
info@findlaymarket.org
www.findlaymarket.org/

———

German Cuisine
6517 Dixie Highway
Florence, Kentucky
Tel.: 859-746-1200

———

Hamman's Butcher Shop, Deli & Catering
6180 Winton Road
Fairfield, Ohio
Tel.: 513-858-3237

———

Jungle Jim's International Market
5440 Dixie Highway
Cincinnati, Ohio
Tel.: 513-674-6000
contactus@junglejims.com
www.junglejims.com/

———

Langen Meats
5855 Cheviot Road
Cincinnati, Ohio
513-385-6600

———

Stehlin's Meat Market
10134 Colerain Avenue
Cincinnati, Ohio
Tel.: 513-574-9033

Wassler's Meat Market
4300 Harrison Avenue
Cincinnati, Ohio
Tel.: 513-574-9033

Hatting's Supermarket
6148 Bridgetown Road
Cincinnati, Ohio
Tel.: 513-574-8660

And, for those interested in an Amish market, there is one located about 45 minutes east of Cincinnati on State Route 32.

Keim's Family Market
2621 Burnt Cabin Road
Seaman, Ohio
Tel.: 937-386-9995

BAKERIES

Two major companies that offer German-style baked goods in the Greater Cincinnati area are the Busken and Servatii bakeries, both of which have branch stores throughout the region.

Busken bakeries are found throughout the region. They are especially well known for their *Schnecken*, which originally were produced and became well known through the former Virginia Bakery that was located in Clifton. Schnecken are described at the Busken Web site (www.busken.com) as follows: "Schnecken simply means 'snail' in German. A schnecken is made by rolling out a flat piece of dough, brushing it liberally with melted butter and adding cinnamon sugar and raisins. It is rolled up into a long 'rope' and cut into slices (that look like snails because of the coils). The slices are baked in a bread mold (three slices per mold) to form a loaf. A schnecken is made with lots of butter. The finished loaf is double wrapped in wax paper and boxed in a special 'Virginia Bakery' box." Listed below are their bakeries by location:

Anderson Township
7754 Beechmont Road
Tel.: 513-232-0615

———

Covedale
5345 Glenway Avenue
Tel.: 513-922-7395

———

Downtown
324 West Ninth Street
Tel.: 513-651-5222

and

800 Walnut Street
Tel.: 513-421-8860

———

Gleneste
956 Old State Route 74
Tel.: 513-753-9540

———

Highland Heights, Kentucky
2895 Alexandria Pike
Tel.: 859-781-5090

———

Hyde Park
2675 Madison Road
Tel.: 513-871-2114
(24 hour bakery)

———

Kenwood
7565 Kendoow Road
Tel.: 513-791-6736

Mason
106 West Main Street
Tel.: 513-398-9787

Milford
Milford Shopping Center
Tel.: 513-831-3350

Norwood
4103 Montgomery Road
Tel.: 513-631-0226

Springdale
370 West Kemper Road
Tel.: 513-671-8454

West Chester
9290 Allen Road
Tel.: 513-942-6350

The Servatii Bakery was founded by Bill Gottenbusch from Muenster in Northern Germany. According to Servatii's Web site (www.servatiipastryshop.com), the bakery is "recognized as the 'Hall of Fame Bakery' in *Cincinnati Magazine*, among the top ten from the state of Ohio, and globally in the first world competition." Listed below are Servatii's bakeries by location:

Anderson Township
7161 Beechmont Avenue
Tel.: 513-231-4455

and

8315 Beechmont Avenue
Tel.: 474-6840

Blue Ash
9525 Kenwood Road
Tel.: 513-791-3013

———

Covedale
2045 Anderson Ferry Road
Tel.: 513-922-0033

———

Downtown
41 East Court Street
Tel.: 513-241-7500

and

35 East Sixth Street
Tel.: 513-421-2253

———

Oakley
3774 Paxton Road
Tel.: 513-871-3244

———

Symmes Township
9130 Montgomery Road
Tel.: 513-469-2277

———

White Oak
5876 Cheviot Road
Tel.: 513-385-3503

Aside from Busken's and Servatii's, the following bakeries also offer German-style baked goods:

Bonomini Bakery
1677 Blue Rock Road
Cincinnati, Ohio
Tel.: 513-541-7501

Entenmann Bakery Outlet
123 W. Kemper Road
Cincinnati, Ohio
Tel.: 513-671-2722

Regina Bakery
4025 Harrison Avenue
Cincinnati, Ohio
Tel.: 513-481-2985

and

3805 Shay Lane
Cincinnati, Ohio
Tel.: 513-941-1585

ICE CREAM

Graeter's was founded by Louis C. Graeter in 1870 and is legendary for its fine ice cream and baked goods. It maintains many stores throughout the greater Cincinnati area, too numerous to list here. For locations, see its Web site.

Graeter's
www.graeters.com

BEER AND WINE

German and German-American beers and wines can be found throughout the area at grocery and state liquor stores, but the following stores have larger selections:

Jungle Jim's International Market
5440 Dixie Highway
Cincinnati, Ohio
Tel.: 513-674-6000
contactus@junglejims.com

Meier's Wine Cellars, Inc.
6955 Plainfield Road

Cincinnati, Ohio
Tel.: 513-229-2900
www.meierswinecellars.com/

———

Party Source
95 Riviera Drive
Bellevue, KY 41073
Tel.: 859-291-4007
www.thepartysource.com/index.php

FLOWERS

Two of the best places to get flowers in Cincinnati, A. J. Rahn's and
Funke's, are located in Wooden Shoe Hollow, so-called because the
German farmers and gardeners wore wooden shoes there. Contact
them as follows:

A. J. Rahn Greenhouses
4944 Gray Road
Cincinnati, Ohio
Tel.: 513-541-0672
www.ajrahngreenhouses.com/whatsNew/index.htm

and

1195 Stone Drive
Harrison, Ohio
Tel.: 513-367-7711

———

Funke's Greenhouses, Inc.
4798 Gray Road
Cincinnati, Ohio
Tel.: 513-541-8170
www.funkes.com/

SPRING GROVE

When visiting Cincinnati, a wonderful place to take a drive or a walk is
Spring Grove Cemetery, which is located just south of Wooden Shoe

Hollow. Many German gardeners worked for, or provided flowers for, Spring Grove. Although it is a cemetery, it also functions as a nature preserve and a park, and is unquestionably one of the most beautiful natural areas in the Greater Cincinnati area, and well worth visiting. The following is an excerpt from the preface of my 1988 edited edition of *Spring Grove and its Creator: H.A. Rattermann's Biography of Adolph Strauch*:

> Spring Grove represents without question one of the finest gems in the crown of the Queen City of the West. A masterpiece of landscaping artistry, it is visited, studied, and admired by thousands each and every year. The beauty of Spring Grove derives from the application of the landscaping design plan, reforms and ideas of Adolph Strauch (1822–83). He described his reforms at Spring Grove as the 'landscape lawn plan,' and called for a return to the 'aesthetics of the beautiful.' In his view a rural cemetery 'should form the most interesting of all places for contemplative recreation; and everything in it should be tasteful, classical, and poetical.' In applying aesthetic principles and design to Spring Grove, Strauch created what is widely considered a masterwork of landscaping art.

For further information about Spring Grove, contact them as follows:

Spring Grove Cemetery and Aboretum
4521 Spring Grove Avenue
Cincinnati, Ohio
Tel.: 513-681-7526
www.springgrove.org

GERMAN GENEALOGICAL SOURCES

For sources relating to German genealogy, see chapter 6, "Libraries and Museums," as well as the "Selective Bibliography" at the end of this volume. For a comprehensive guide to regional sources, see Connie Stunkel Terheiden and Kenny R. Burck, *A Guide to Genealogical Resources in Cincinnati & Hamilton County, Ohio*. 5th Edition (Milford: Little Miami Publishing Co., 2006). Visit the chapter's Web site at the following address:

Hamilton County Genealogical Society
www.hcgsohio.org/

Book Stores

A variety of bookstores exist in the Greater Cincinnati area, including chain and specialty stores, as well as museum shops that carry books on local and regional history. This list also includes shops that carry new and used German-language books such as Aims, Duttenhofer's, and the Ohio Book Store.

Aims Foreign Language Books
7709 Hamilton Avenue
Cincinnati, OH 45231
Tel.: 513-521-5590

—————

B. Dalton Books
For store locations see
www.barnesandnoble.com

—————

Barnes and Noble Books
For store location see
www.barnesandnoble.com

—————

Borders Books
For store locations see
www.bordersstores.com

—————

Cincinnati Museum Center
Store to Explore
1301 Western Avenue.
Cincinnati, Ohio 45203-1130
Tel.: 800-733-2077
www.cincymuseum.org

—————

Duttenhofer's Books & News
214 West McMillan Street
Cincinnati, Ohio 45219-1309
Tel.: 513-381-1340

German Heritage Museum
4764 West Fork Road
Cincinnati, Ohio
Tel.: 513-598-5732
www.gacl.org

Joseph-Beth Booksellers
2692 Madison Road
Cincinnati, Ohio 45208
Tel.: 513-396-8960
www.josephbeth.com

Little Miami Publishing Co.
19 Water Street
P.O. Box 588
Milford, Ohio 45150
Tel.: 513-576-9369
www.littlemiamibooks.com

Ohio Book Store
726 Main Street
Cincinnati, Ohio 45202
Tel.: 513-621-5142

Significant Books
P.O. Box 9248
Cincinnati, Ohio 45209
Tel.: 513-321-7567
www.significantbooks.com

Waldenbooks
www.waldenbooks.com

NOTES

Introduction

1. Henry Howe, *Historical Collections of Ohio*, 2 vols. (Cincinnati: C. J. Krehbiel & Co., 1907), 847.
2. Lewis A. Leonard, *Greater Cincinnati and its People: A History*. (New York: Lewis Historical Publishing Co., 1927), 1:104. Leonard also writes of the Cincinnati Germans: "No class of people have contributed more . . . than the Germans. And no class is entitled to greater credit. They are modest and retiring in their disposition, not given to brag or bluster, and make no boisterous claims of what they have accomplished, but are content to plod along in the paths of industry, and let their work tell the stranger what they have accomplished," 105.

Chapter 1

1. George A. Katzenberger, *The First Mayor of Cincinnati: George A. Katzenberger's Biography of Major David Ziegler*. ed. by Don Heinrich Tolzmann. (Lanham, Md.: University Press of America, 1990), 43.
2. Ibid, 48. Ziegler was first buried in the old Presbyterian cemetery on the Fourth Street front, which then became a business district, and so he was moved to the cemetery which is now Washington Park in Over-the-Rhine. After the Woodland Cemetery opened in Dayton, the remains of Mrs. Ziegler and her husband were moved to there, as Mrs. Ziegler had moved to Dayton.
3. Howe, *Historical Collections*, 1:127.
4. Johann Heckewelder, *The First Description of Cincinnati and other Ohio Settlements: The Travel Report of Johann Heckewelder (1792)* ed. Don Heinrich Tolzmann. (Lanham, Md.: University Press of America, 1988), 42–45. Heckewelder was not entirely positive in his remarks, and provided the following critique of the early settlement: "The town is overrun with merchants and traders and overstocked with merchandise; there are already over 30 stores and warehouses here, and the one ruins the others. Idlers are plentiful here, according to the assertion of the respectable people a multitude like the Sodomites. It is however hoped, that the place, as well as the other settlements on the north side of the Ohio, will in the course of time, and probably soon, be cleared of this bad element, for experience teaches, that as soon as they are brought under the hands of the law, they seek the shores of Kentucky (which lies directly across the Ohio), and if

they are caught there, they escape to the extreme borders of the Clinch or Cumberland river, or even to Orleans," 45.

5. Don Heinrich Tolzmann, ed., *Das Ohiotal—The Ohio Valley: The German Dimension* (New York: Peter Lang Pub. Co., 1993), 167.

6. Howe, *Historical Collections*, 2:855.

7. Don Heinrich Tolzmann, "Recovery and Reconstruction," pt. 3 of *Cincinnati's German Heritage* (Bowie, Md.: Heritage Books, Inc., 1994), 4.

8. Ibid.

9. Emil Klauprecht, *The German Chronicle*, 170.

10. Don Heinrich Tolzmann, ed., *Festschrift for the German-American Tricentennial Jubilee: Cincinnati 1983* (Cincinnati: Cincinnati Historical Society, 1982), 4.

11. Tolzmann, *Das Ohiotal*, 170.

12. Emil Klauprecht, *The German Chronicle in the History of the Ohio Valley and its Capital City, Cincinnati, in Particular*, trans. Dale V. Lally, ed. by Don Heinrich Tolzmann. (Bowie, Md.: Heritage Books, Inc., 1992), 177.

13. Regarding nativism, see Klauprecht, *The German Chronicle*, 176–193.

14. Klauprecht, *The German Chronicle*, 179.

15. Tolzmann, *Festschrift*, 3.

16. Klauprecht, *The German Chronicle*, 186.

17. Don Heinrich Tolzmann, ed., *The German-American Forty-Eighters, 1848–1998.* (Indianapolis: Max Kade German-American Center, Indiana University-Purdue University at Indianapolis & Indiana German Heritage Society, 1998), 98, 105.

18. Klauprecht comments that: "The bloody Know-Nothingism had a positive effect on the German population, in that the Germans drew together even more than before." See Klauprecht, *The German Chronicle*, 193.

19. Regarding Gerstaecker's stay in Cincinnati, see Klauprecht, *The German Chonicle*, 176.

20. "Lincoln Visited by a German Delegation of Workingmen in Cincinnati, Ohio, February 12, 1861," *Lincoln Lore*. no. 1575 (May 1969), 2.

21. Regarding Stallo, see Henry A. Ford, *The History of Cincinnati, Ohio, With Illustrations and Biographical Sketches* (Cincinnati: L. A. Williams & Co., 1881), 143-46.

22. *Children's May Festival, Cincinnati Music Hall: Under the Auspices of the German-American Free Kindergarten Association, Saturday, May 1st and 8th, 1897, Frank van der Stucken, Musical Director* (Cincinnati: Cincinnati Symphony Orchestra, 1897), 24.

23. Don Heinrich Tolzmann, *Covington's German Heritage* (Bowie, Md.: Heritage Books, Inc., 1998), 49.

24. Robert Heuck II, *Hubert Heuck and His Opera Houses* (Cincinnati: Florence McKee Heuck, 1992), 43.

25. John Robertson, *The Last Strike for Liberty: A Semi-Political Satire on the Revolutionary Demands of the Liberal Foreign Element* (Cincinnati: Published for the Author, 1886), 3, 8.

26. Tolzmann, *Festschrift*, 87.

27. A. H. Walburg, *German Language and Literature* (Columbus, Ohio: Printed at the Josephinium, 1896), 26–27.

28. John Lewin McLeish, *The Americanization Problem in Cincinnati* (Cincinnati: American Art Printing Co., 1921).

29. Tolzmann, *Festschrift*, 97.

30. From 1939 onwards, the platform appeared on a regular basis in the newspaper.

31. Cincinnati Central Turners, *Gems in Gymnastics, 1848–1941* (Covington, Ky.: Wolff Printing Co., 1941), 22.

32. *The Cincinnati Post*, 13 March 1939. See Don Heinrich Tolzmann, *Thomas Mann in Cincinnati* Max Kade Occasional Papers in German-American Studies. (Cincinnati: German-American Studies Program, University of Cincinnati, 2003).

33. Public Library of Cincinnati and Hamilton County, *Prosit Cincinnati*, (Cincinnati: Public Library of Cincinnati and Hamilton Co., 1976), n.p.

34. For Reagan's proclamation, see Don Heinrich Tolzmann, *The German-American Experience* (Amherst, N.Y.: Humanity Books, 2000), 365–66.

Chapter 2

1. This list was compiled and extracted from sources listed in the selective bibliography, especially part three, which lists general works dealing with the history of Cincinnati in general, and the Cincinnati Germans in particular.

2. Don Heinrich Tolzmann, *Festschrift for the German-American Tricentennial Jubilee: Cincinnati 1983* (Cincinnati: Cincinnati Historical Society, 1982) 4.

Chapter 3

1. For biographical information on the Cincinnati Germans, see the biographical indexes listed in part two of the selective bibliography.

2. See World Wide Web <http://enquirer.com/editions/1999/10/27/loc_famous_engraving_of.html>.

Chapter 4

1. This list of historic sites in the Over-the-Rhine is a selection drawn from my tour guide to Over-the-Rhine, which is at the Web site of the German-American Studies Program at the University of Cincinnati. See World Wide Web <http://asweb.artsci.uc.edu/german/geram.htm>.

Chapter 5

1. The sites listed in this chapter are drawn from my book, *Covington's German Heritage*. (Bowie, Md.: Heritage Books, Inc., 1998).

Chapter 6

1. For a guide to area libraries see the Web site of the Greater Cincinnati Library Consortium. See World Wide Web <http://www.gclc-lib.org>.

Chapter 7

1. The GACL Web site lists all of the member societies, and also provides an annual calendar of events. Its newspaper, *German-American Chronicle of the Ohio Valley*, also provides this information and is available at the German houses in the area. See World Wide Web <www.gacl.org>.

SELECTIVE BIBLIOGRAPHY

Bibliographical Sources

Arndt, Karl J. R. and May E. Olson. *The German Language Press of the Americas*. München: K. G. Saur, 1976–80.

Cincinnati Historical Society Library. *Nippert Collection of German Methodism, 1779–1974*. Cincinnati: Cincinnati Historical Society, 1995.

Ott, Franziska C. *Cincinnati German Imprints*. New York: Peter Lang Pub. Co., 1993.

Terheiden, Connie Stunkel and Kenny R. Burck. *Guide to Genealogical Resources in Cincinnati and Hamilton County, Ohio*. Cincinnati: Hamilton County Chapter of the Ohio Genealogical Society, 2001.

Tolzmann, Don Heinrich. *Catalog of the German-Americana Collection, University of Cincinnati*. 2 vols. München: K.G. Saur, 1990.

_____. *German-Americana: A Bibliography*. Metuchen, N.J.: Scarecrow Press, 1975; Bowie, Md.: Heritage Books, Inc., 1994.

_____. *German-Americana Collection: Inventories to the Collections*. Cincinnati: University of Cincinnati Libraries, Archives and Rare Books Department, 1998– .

Biographical Indexes

Andrusko, Samuel M. *Der Deutsche Pionier: Membership Lists (1869–1887) of the Deutschen Pionier-Vereins of Cincinnati and its Branches in Dayton and Toledo (Ohio) and Covington and Newport (Kentucky), With Selected Additional Biographical Information and Obituaries and Biographies in the Deutschen Pionier*. Washington, D.C.: S. M. Andrusko, 1989.

Herbert, Jeffrey C. *Index of Death and Other Notices Appearing in the Cincinnati Freie Presse, 1874–1920*. Bowie, Md.: Heritage Books, Inc., 1993.

_____. *Index of Death Lists Appearing the Cincinnatier Zeitung, 1887–1901*. Bowie, Md.: Heritage Books, Inc., 1999.

_____. *Index of Death Notices and Marriage Notices Appearing in the Cincinnati Volksfreund, 1850–1908*. Bowie, Md.: Heritage Books, Inc., 1991.

_____. *Index of Death Notices Appearing in the Cincinnati Volksblatt, 1846–1918*. Bowie, Md.: Heritage Books, Inc., 1998.

_____, trans. *Translated Abstracts of Death Notices in the Portsmouth Correspondent, 1894–1908*. Edited by Barbara Keyser Gargiulo. Milford, Ohio: Little Miami Pub., 2000.

Hughes, Lois. *Hamilton County, Ohio Citizenship Record Abstracts, 1837–1916.* Bowie, Md.: Heritage Books, Inc., 1991.

Tolzmann, Don Heinrich. *The Ohio Valley German Biographical Index.* Bowie, Md.: Heritage Books, Inc., 1992, and *Supplement,* 1993.

General Works

Chambrun, Clara Longworth. *Cincinnati: Story of the Queen City.* New York: Scribner, 1939.

Cincinnati Art Museum. *Celebrate Cincinnati Art: In Honor of the One Hundredth Anniversary of the Cincinnati Art Museum, 1881–1981.* Cincinnati: The Museum, 1982.

Cincinnati Historic Conservation Office. *Over-the-Rhine (South) Historic District: Designation Report.* Cincinnati: Historic Conservation Office, 1993.

Cincinnati Symphony Orchestra. *Cincinnati Symphony Orchestra: Centennial Portraits.* Cincinnati: Cincinnati Symphony Orchestra, 1994.

Clubbe, John. *Cincinnati Observed: Architecture and History.* Columbus: Ohio State University Press, 1992.

Duveneck, Josephine W. *Frank Duveneck: Painter-Teacher.* San Francisco: John Howell-Books, 1970.

Easton, Loy D. *Hegel's First American Followers: The Ohio Hegelians: John B. Stallo, Peter Kaufmann, Moncure Conway, and August Willich, With Key Writings.* Athens: Ohio University Press, 1966.

Ehrlinger, David. *The Cincinnati Zoo and Botanical Garden.* Cincinnati: Cincinnati Zoo and Botanical Garden, 1993.

Federal Writers' Project (Ohio). *They Built a City: 150 Years of Industrial Cincinnati.* Cincinnati: The Cincinnati Post, 1938.

Ford, Henry Allen. *History of Cincinnati, Ohio, With Illustrations and Biographical Sketches.* Cleveland: L. A. Williams & Co., 1881.

Giglierano, Geoffrey J. et al. *The Bicentennial Guide to Greater Cincinnati: A Portrait of Two Hundred Years.* Cincinnati: Cincinnati Historical Society, 1988.

Goss, Charles F. *Cincinnati, the Queen City, 1788–1912.* 4 vols. Chicago: S. J. Clarke Pub. Co., 1912.

Grace, Kevin and Tom White. *Cincinnati Revealed: A Photographic Heritage of the Queen City.* Chicago: Arcadia Pub. Co., 2002.

Grebner, Constantin. *We Were the Ninth: A History of the Ninth Regiment, Ohio Volunteer Infantry, April 17, 1861, to June 7, 1864.* Edited by Frederic Trautmann. Kent, Ohio: Kent State University Press, 1987.

Greve, Charles T. *Centennial History of Cincinnati and Representative Citizens.* Chicago: Biographical Pub. Co., 1904.

Harlow, Alvin F. *The Serene Cincinnatians.* (New York: Dutton, 1950).

Heckewelder, Johann. *The First Description of Cincinnati and Other Ohio Settlements: The Travel Report of Johann Heckewelder (1792), With an Introduction by H. A. Rattermann.* Edited by Don Heinrich Tolzmann. Lanham, Md.: University Press of America, 1988.

History of Cincinnati and Hamilton County, Ohio: Their Past and Present, Including Early Settlement and Development, Antiquarian Researches, Their Aboriginal History, Pioneer History, Political Organization, Agricultural, Mining and Manufacturing Interests, a History of the City, Villages and Townships, Religious, Educational, Social, Military and Political History, Statistics, Biographies and Portraits of Pioneers and Representative Citizens, etc.: Cincinnati: S. B. Nelson, 1894.

Holian, Timothy J. *The German-Americans and World War II: An Ethnic Experience.* New York: Peter Lang Pub. Co., 1996.

_____. *Over the Barrel: The Brewing History and Beer Culture of Cincinnati.* 2 vols. St. Joseph, Mo.: Sudhaus Press, 2000.

Hurley, Daniel. *Cincinnati, the Queen City.* Cincinnati: Cincinnati Historical Society, 1982.

Katzenberger, George A. *The First Mayor of Cincinnati: George A. Katzenberger's Biography of Major David Ziegler.* Edited by Don Heinrich Tolzmann. Lanham, Md.: University Press of America, 1990.

Kaufmann, Wilhelm. *The Germans in the American Civil War: With A Biographical Directory.* Edited by Don Heinrich Tolzmann et al. Carlisle, Pa.: John Kallmann, 1999.

Klauprecht, Emil. *Cincinnati, or, the Mysteries of the West: Emil Klauprecht's German-American Novel.* Translated by Steven Rowan and Edited by Don Heinrich Tolzmann. New York: Peter Lang Pub. Co., 1996.

_____ *German Chronicle in the History of the Ohio Valley, and its Capital City Cincinnati, in Particular.* Translated by Dale Lally, Jr. and Edited by Don Heinrich Tolzmann. Bowie, Md.: Heritage Books, Inc., 1992.

Kleber, John, ed. *The Kentucky Encyclopedia.* Lexington: University Press of Kentucky, 1991.

Kraut, Benny. *German Jewish Orthodoxy in an Immigrant Synagogue: Cincinnati's New Hope Congregation and the Ambiguities of Ethnic Religion.* New York: M. Wiener Pub., 1988.

Kraemer, Albert O. *Kraemer's Picturesque Cincinnati.* Cincinnati: A. O. and G. A. Kraemer, 1898; Cincinnati: Ohio Book Store, 1985.

Langsam, Walter E. *Great Houses of the Queen City: Two Hundred Years of Historic and Contemporary Architecture and Interiors in Cincinnati and Northern Kentucky.* Cincinnati: Cincinnati Historical Society, 1997.

Leonard, Lewis A. *Greater Cincinnati and its People: A History.* New York: Lewis Historical Publishing Co., 1927.

Lippert, Thomas J. *Leon Lippert: Rediscovering the Art and the Man.* Cincinnati: ArtLeaf Publishing Co., 2001.

Miller, Zane. *Boss Cox's Cincinnati: Urban Politics in the Progressive Era.* New York: Oxford University Press, 1968.

Miller, Zane and George F. Roth. *Cincinnati's Music Hall.* Virginia Beach, Va.; Jordan & Co., 1978.

Peck, Abraham J. and Uri D. Herscher, eds., *Queen City Refuge: An Oral History of Cincinnati's Jewish Refugees from Nazi Germany.* West Orange, N.J.: Behrman House, 1989.

Perry, Dick. *Vas You Ever in Zinzinnati?* New York: Weathervane, 1966.

Poole, William Frederick. *The Tyler Davidson Fountain: Given by Mr. Henry Probasco to the City of Cincinnati.* 1872. Reprint, Cincinnati: Cincinnati Historical Society, 1986.

Rattermann, H. A. *Kentucky's German Pioneers: H. A. Rattermann's History.* Edited by Don Heinrich Tolzmann. Bowie, Md.: Heritage Books, Inc. 2001.

_____. *Spring Grove and Its Creator: H. A. Rattermann's Biography of Adolph Strauch.* Edited by Don Heinrich Tolzmann. Cincinnati: The Ohio Book Store, 1988)

Roe, George M. *Cincinnati: The Queen City of the West: Her Principal Men and Institutions, Biographical Sketches, and Portraits of Leading Citizens, Descriptive Accounts of her Enterprises.* Cincinnati: Cincinnati Times-Star Co; Press of C. J. Krehbiel & Co., 1895.

Sheblessey, Sylvia Kleve. *100 Years of the Cincinnati May Festival.* Cincinnati, N.p. 1973.

Silverstein, Iola Hessler. *Cincinnati, Then and Now.* Cincinnati: League of Women's Voters of the Cincinnati Area, 1982.

Springer, Annemarie. Nineteenth Century German-American Church Artists. 2001. http://www.ulib.iupui.edu/kade/springer/index.html.

Tenkotte, Paul Allen. *A Heritage of Art and Faith: Downtown Covington Churches.* Covington, Ky.: Kenton County Historical Society, 1986.

Tolzmann, Don Heinrich. *Cincinnati's German Heritage.* Bowie, Md.: Heritage Books, Inc., 1994.

_____. *Covington's German Heritage.* Bowie, Md.: Heritage Books, Inc., 1998.

_____, ed. *Festschrift for the German-American Tricentennial Jubilee, Cincinnati 1983.* The Cincinnati Historical Society Studies in Regional and Local History. No. 2 Cincinnati: Cincinnati Historical Society, 1982.

_____. *The John R. Roebling Suspension Bridge on the Ohio River.* Max Kade Occasional Papers in German-American Studies, No. 1. Cincinnati: German-American Studies Program, University of Cincinnati, 1998.

_____. *Ohio's German Heritage.* Bowie, Md.: Heritage Books, Inc., 2002.

_____. *Das Ohiotal–The Ohio Valley: the German Dimension.* New York: Peter Lang Pub. Co., 1992.

Toth, Carolyn. *German-English Bilingual Schools in America: The Cincinnati Tradition in Historical Context.* New York: Peter Lang Pub. Co., 1990.

Vitz, Robert C. *The Queen and the Arts: The Cultural Life in Nineteenth-Century Cincinnati.* Kent, Ohio: Kent State University Press, 1989.

Wilson, John. *American Paintings at Procter & Gamble: The Historic Cincinnati Collection.* Cincinnati: Procter & Gamble, 1999.

Wimberg, Robert J. *Cincinnati: Over-the-Rhine: A Historical Guide to 19th Century Buildings and Their Residents.* Cincinnati: Ohio Book Store, 1987.

Wittke, Carl. *William Nast, Patriarch of German Methodism.* Detroit: Wayne State University Press, 1959.

INDEX

A

A Refutation of the Versailles War Guilt Thesis (Wegerer) 34
A. Koehnken and Grimm 52, 93
AADUV 110
Academy of Art 7
Academy of Fine Art 67
ADUV 110
Ahrens Manufacturing Co. 67
Ahrens, Chris 67
Aims Foreign Language Books 132
Albers, Hermann 108
Alger, Horatio 57
Allgemeiner Deutscher Unterstuetzungs Verein 110
Alms
    family 24
    Frederick 83
    William 83
Alms and Doepke Building 83
Alpen Echos (band) 116
Alsace-Lorraine, France/Germany 7, 47
Altenheim 24
American Bicentennial 36
American Citizens League 104
American House 31
Americanization Executive Committee 31
Americanization Problem in Cincinnati, The 31
Amerikanische Buerger-Liga 104
Amerika-Woche 37, 114, 115
Amos Shinkle Townhouse, the 95
Andrews Soap Co. 22, 78
Ankum, Germany 39, 57
anti-German hysteria 30, 61, 63, 92, 93, 104
Archbishop's Church 16
Art Academy of Cincinnati 57, 96
Athenaeum 7
Atlantic Garden 18
Austro-Hungarian Empire 31
Avril & Bleh Meat Market 123

B

B. Dalton Books 132
B'nai Yeshrum 12
bakeries
    Bonomini Bakery 128
    Busken 125, 126, 127
    Entenmann Bakery Outlet 129
    Regina Bakery 129
    Servatii 125, 127, 128
    Virginia Bakery 125
Baltimore, Maryland 47
    port city of 4
banking 59
Baptisten Kirche 83
Barber's Local Union 51
Barbers, Cincinnati German 51
barge
    Cincinnati, speed record 7
Barnes and Noble Books 132
Barnhorn, Clement H. 88, 96, 97
Battle of
    Chickamauga 55
    Hermann/*Hermannsschlacht*, major nativist riot 12
    Lexington 48
    Missionary Ridge 55
    Perryville 55
    Shiloh 55
Baum, Martin 4, 6, 47, 67, 100
Baur, Clara 57, 67
Bauvereine 59
Bavaria, Germany 64
Bavarian Beneficial Society 40
Bavarian Brewing Co. 26, 94
Bedini Riot 15
Bedini, Papal Nuncio 15
Beech Acres 14
beer and wine 129
    Jungle Jim's International Market 129
    Meier's Wine Cellars, Inc. 129
    Party Source 130
beer consumption 25
Behm, Heinrich 6
Behringer-Crawford Museum 100
Benninghofen House 101
Bericht über eine Reise nach den westlichen Staaten Nordamerika (Duden) 8
Berlin Airlift 39
Berlin Street 61
Berlin, Germany 20, 52, 55
Bernstorff, Count Johann Heinrich von 29
Bethesda Hospital 43

Bismarck, Otto von 19
Black Forest Restaurant 62, 120
Blegen Library, University of Cincinnati
    102
blue laws 23
Bluecher, Prince 10
Blum, Robert F. 67
Board of Education 20
Bode, August 104
Bonomini Bakery 128
book stores 132
    Aims Foreign Language Books 132
    B. Dalton Books 132
    Barnes and Noble Books 132
    Borders Books 132
    Cincinnati Museum Center (Store to Ex-
        plore) 132
    Duttenhofer's Books & News 132
    German Heritage Museum 133
    Joseph-Beth Booksellers 133
    Little Miami Publishing Co. 133
    Ohio Book Store 133
    Significant Books 133
    Waldenbooks 133
bootleggers 31
    arrests 32
Borders Books 132
Boss Cox machine 71
Brau Haus 121
brewers
    Burger 36
    Hauck, John, Brewing Co. 26
    Hudepohl 36
    Schoenling 36
    Wiedemann 36
Brooklyn Bridge 19, 55, 95
Brotzeit Deli 120
Brown County Historical Society Museum
    (New Ulm, Minn.) 14
Bruckmann, John C., Brewery 26
Buerger-Liga 104
Buffalo, Wisconsin 14
Burgheim, Max 22
Burkhalter, Christian 10
Butler County Historical Society 101

C

Camp Dennison 5, 48, 49
candle and soap-making 9
Carroll Chimes Bell Tower 63
Carroll, Julian 63
Cathedral Basilica, the 96
Central Turners
    oldest German society 13
Chester Park 27
Chicago, Illinois 37
Children's Hospital 25

Children's May Festival 20
Christian Moerlein Brewing Co. 26, 44
Christian Moerlein Building 81
Christliche Apologete, Der 12
Church of the Steps 16, 76
Cincinnati 7
Cincinnati Art Museum 99
Cincinnati Butcher Supply Co. 76
Cincinnati Central Turners 104
Cincinnati City Council 61
Cincinnati first Oktoberfest 36
Cincinnati Freie Presse 34
Cincinnati German Barbers 51
Cincinnati German Imprints, A Checklist
    (Ott) 40
Cincinnati Historical Society Library 101
Cincinnati History Museum and Historical
    Society 100
Cincinnati in Color (Langsam) 36
Cincinnati Kolping Center 109
Cincinnati Kurier 37, 108
Cincinnati Kurier, Der 114
Cincinnati Millacron, Inc. 68
Cincinnati Museum Center 101, 132
Cincinnati Old Men's Home 24
Cincinnati Pops Orchestra 41, 73
Cincinnati Public Schools 36
    German bilingual program 30
    German Department 68
Cincinnati Reds 71, 76
    Opening Day 82
Cincinnati Schnapps Band 116
Cincinnati Schuetzen-Verein 19
Cincinnati Strong Man 71
Cincinnati Symphony Orchestra 57, 72, 76,
    77, 80, 103
Cincinnati Turner Colonization Society 105
Cincinnati Turnverein 14, 53, 54
Cincinnati USA & Visitors Bureau 113
Cincinnati Valve Company 64
Cincinnati Volksblatt 53, 76
Cincinnati Zoo 20, 22, 25, 56, 67, 77
Cincinnati's Classical Public Radio 116
Cincinnati, City of 36, 40
Cincinnati, Ohio 36, 39, 41, 51, 55
    military district of 55
Cincinnati, or the Mysteries of the West
    (Klauprecht) 72
Cincinnati's Bicentennial 52
Cincinnati's first
    beer garden 7
    city council prints ordinances in German
        12
    decorated Christmas tree 10
    description of area published in Germany
        5
    gardener 6

German artist 7
German Catholic newspaper (and first in
  the United States) 11
German Catholic priest 7, 76
German congregation in Cincinnati 7
German daily newspaper 10
German newspaper 8
German plays 13
German publication 6
German sermons 6
German society in Cincinnati 7
German-American archbishop 27
German-American congregation 79
German-language public school 12
Maifest 13
major nativist riot 12
mayor 3, 6
Oktoberfest Zinzinnati 36
ornamental garden 4
private German-language school 7
public library 5
Turner Society 13
Cincinnati's German Heritage
  historical marker 41
Cincinnati's oldest German-style festival 19
Cincinnati's Original Oktoberfest 108
Civil War 5
  18, 20, 54, 74
  veterans 19
Clifton Heights, Ohio 30, 63
Clifton, Ohio 7
Coburg, Germany
  Duchess of 20
College of Music 57
Columbia University 32
Concordia Lutheran Church 35, 84, 119
Coney Island 34
Conservatory of Music 57, 67
Corryville, Ohio 22, 61
Covington Altar Build Stock Co. (Institute
  of Catholic Art) 18
Covington and Cincinnati Bridge Co. 56, 95
Covington Turners 93, 105, 106
Covington, Kentucky 7, 19, 37, 55, 62, 63,
  68, 89, 93, 97, 100
Covington, Ky. 13
Covington, Leonard 7
Covington's Institute of Catholic Art 57, 96

D

Danube Swabian Day 35
Day of German Unity 40
Day, Doris (nee Kappelhoff) 67
Dayton, Ohio 3
Deaconess Hospital 23, 24
Deer Creek, Ohio 4
Deglow Brewing Co. 94

Der Wahrheitsfreund 11
Deschwanden, Paul 93
Deutsch-Amerikanische Buerger-Liga 104
Deutsche Evangelisch Reformierte Salems
  Kirche 82
Deutsche Evangelische Paulus Kirche 84
Deutsche Gegenseitige Versicherungs-Ge-
  sellschaft von Cincinnati 83
Deutsche Pionier, Der 19, 21, 58
Deutsche Protestantische Sankt Johannes
  Kirche 79
Deutsche Tag-Gesellschaft 104
Deutscher Hausverein 110
Deutscher Tag 103
Devou Park 100
Diakonissen Krankenhaus 23
Doepke, William 83
Donauschwaben Society events
  Donauschwaben Day 107
  Kirchweih 107
  Oktoberfest 107
  Strauss Ball 107
Donauschwaben, immigration of the 35
Donnenfelser 93
Doorn, Holland 72
Duchess of Coburg 20
Duden, Gottfried 8
Duke Wilhelm V of Bavaria 41
Duttenhofer's Books & News 132
Duveneck
  Frank 17, 52, 57, 67, 74, 92, 96, 97
  House 96
  Monument 97

E

Eckstein, Friedrich 67
Eden Park 99
Eine Rheinreise, Cincinnati's first German-
  American radio program 32
Elberfeld, Germany 109
Elfferrat, the 108
Elm Street School 81
Emery Auditorium 32
Emphasis>History of Cincinnati (Ford) 1
Engel, Marie Lammers 108
English Lutheran Church 85
English Street 61
Entenmann Bakery Outlet 129
Erkenbrecher
  Andrew 20, 56, 67
  family 24
Erler, Gebhard 119
Ernst
  Franz Josef 78
  John P. 96
  William 96
Ernst Home 96

Eschenlohr, Wolfgang 116
Evangelical Protestant Society for Deacon-
ess Work and Care for the Sick 23
Evangelisch Protestantischer Verein fuer
Diakonie 23
Evangelisch-Lutherische Dreifaltigkeits-
Gemeinde 84

F

Fairview German Language School 36, 63
Fairview Heights Park 61
Fairview Park, Clifton Heights 30, 40
Faust, Albert B. 34
Federal Republic of Germany 36
Federation of German-American Workers'
Singing Societies 36
festivals
Christkindlmarkt 114
German Day 114
German-American Heritage Month 114
Oktoberfest 114
Saengerfest 114
Schuetzenfest 114
St. Nikolaus Day 114
Fettweis, Leopold 53, 68
Fick, Heinrich H. 36, 68, 69, 80, 103
Findlay Market 30, 81, 82, 124
Findlay, James 81
first
bilingual public school 70
German settlement in America, bicenten-
nial of the 22
German-American governor of Kentucky
68
steam flouring mill 4
vineyard 4
woolen factory 4
*First Description of Cincinnati and Other
Ohio Settlement, The* 5
First English Lutheran Church 85
first paper mill in Ohio 48
first permanent German settlement 64
First Presbyterian Church 72
First World War 61, 63, 71, 72, 80, 84, 92,
93, 104
Fleischmann Yeast Co. 68
Fleischmann, Julius 68
flowers
A. J. Rahn Greenhouses 130
Funke's Greenhouses, Inc. 130
Fort Washington 48
Forty-eighters 15
immigration of 13
Forty-first National Saengerfest 36
Fountain Square 56, 64
Franco-Prussian War 19
Frankenstein

Gottfried 68
Johann Peter 68
Franz Klaber Orchestra 118
Fraundorfer, George 62
free lunch tradition 19
Freie Presse 29
Friedrich Hecker Monument 53
Friedrich Jahn Memorial Monument 52
Friedrich, Eckstein 7
Froebel, Friedrich 20
Frost, Jack 119
Funke's Greenhouses, Inc. 130

G

Galvin, John 28
Gebhard Erler Duo 119
Geier, Frederick A. 68
General Electric 74
George Wiedemann Brewing Co. 26
German 30
German Ambassador 29
German Bakers Singing Society 86
German Baptist Church 83
German bilingual program 30
German bilingual school 36, 63, 80
*German Chronicle in the History of the
Ohio Valley, and its Capital City, Cincin-
nati, in Particular* (Klauprecht) 72
German church services
Concordia Lutheran Church 119
Old St. Mary's Church 119
German Cuisine 121, 124
German Day 22, 36, 37, 58, 103
first annual 25
German Day Society 25, 104
German Deaconess Home and Hospital 23
German Department
Cincinnati Public Schools 36
University of Cincinnati 26, 34
German Federation of Hamilton 110
German genealogical sources 131
German General Protestant Orphan Home
13
German gifts
Christkindlmarkt 120
Germania Society 120
Linden Noll Gift Haus 120
Oktoberfest 120
Saxony Imports 120
German Gothic Glockenspiel 63
German Haydn Society 7
German Heritage Museum 51, 99, 103, 133
grand opening 40
German immigrants 9
German Jews 12, 32
German Kolping Society 84
German Language and Literature (Wal-

burg) 25
German Literary Club 22, 31, 86
German Lutheran Reformed Church 7
German Lutherans 84
German Methodist Church 74
German Moravian missionary 5
German Mutual Insurance Co. 57, 75, 83, 84
German National Bank 59, 61, 96
German Orphan Home 13
German Pioneer Society 19, 21, 31, 32, 78
German Reading and Cultural Society 13
German Reformed Church 82, 93
German regiment (Civil War) 74
German Revolution of 1848 13, 15, 53, 54, 55
German singing societies 51
German Society (mutual aid society) 9
German Street 61
German street names, changes to 30, 61
German television 119
German theater 105
German Tunes of the Queen City 42, 115
German Turner Society 105
German unification, local support for 19
German Village Historic District (Hamilton, Ohio) 101
German-American Alliance 25, 27, 104
German-American bands 116
  Alpen Echos 116, 118
  Cincinnati Schnapps Band 116
  Franz Klaber Orchestra 118
  Gebhard Erler Duo 119
  Jack Frost Accordion Band 119
  Nick Gulacsy 116
  Pete Wagner Band 118
  Polka Dots 119
  Pros't Band 118
German-American book publishing 40
German-American Chronicle of the Ohio Valley, The 41, 103
German-American Citizens League 40, 51, 58, 103, 104, 114
German-American Combined Singers 32, 35
German-American Day 37, 39, 40, 56, 74
German-American Federation of Singing Societies 51
German-American Free Kindergarten Association 20
German-American Friendship Garden 39
German-American Heritage Month 39, 64, 103
German-American News 41
German-American newspapers 70
  Amerika-Woche 114, 115
  Der Cincinnati Kurier 114
  German-American News 114

German-American population move
  northern Kentucky 26
  West side Cincinnati 26
German-American radio programs 42
  German Tunes of the Queen City 115
  International Program 115
  Melodies of German & Austria Program 115
  Mid-Morning with Wolf 116
  Over-the-Rhine Showcase 115
German-American Regiments in the Civil War 54
German-American Relief for Germany Committee 35
German-American singing societies 57, 58
German-American societies 51, 103
German-American Studies Program 37, 40
German-American Tricentennial 37
German-American Week 36
German-American, internment of 34
German-Americana Collection 36, 68, 102
German-Austro-Hungarian Aid Society 29, 30
German-bilingual kindergarten 20
German-English Normal School 20
German-English School 70
Germania 84
Germania Brewing Co. 26
Germania Building 58, 75, 83, 84
Germania Park 40
Germania Society 36, 107, 108, 120
German-language instruction
  prohibition of 31
Germantown, Penn. 22, 32, 37, 64
Germantowne Pizza Haus 121
Germany (later known as Camp Dennison) 5
Germany, Ohio 48, 49
Gerstaecker, Friedrich 16
Gesellenverein 109
glass door oven, first 43, 72
Glier's 41
Glockenspiel 63
Goebel Park 63, 68, 91
Goebel, William 63, 68
goetta 41
Goetz
  house 62
  John 62
Gold Club 109
Good Friday Pilgrimage 17
Goose Girl Fountain, the 63, 89
Gottenbusch, Bill 127
Grace United Church of Christ 93
Graeter, Louis C. 68, 129
Grammer, Anton 86, 87
Grammer, Frank, Jr. 87

Grammer's Restaurant 20, 86
Grant, Ulysses S. 78
Greater Cincinnati and its People
A History (Leonard) 1
Green Township 51
Greene Lodge 104
Grimm (see A. Koehnken and Grimm) 52, 93
Grimm Brothers 63, 89
Gulacsy, Nick 116
Guttenberg, Iowa 14

H

Hagenau, Germany 4, 47
Hallelujah Chorous 7
Hambacher Fest 10, 13
Hamilton Mutual Insurance Company 58
Hamilton, Ohio 101
Hamman's Butcher Shop, Deli & Catering 124
Hannover, Germany 57
Hardman, Gregory 44
Hassaurek, Friedrich 53, 69
Hatting's Supermarket 125
Hauck
    Dr. Frederick 69
    John 22, 59, 69, 99
Hauck beer
    Export Lager 59
    Invalid Beer 59
    John Hauck Golden Eagle Lager 59
    Pilsner 59
    SuperFine 59
Hauck House Museum 59, 69, 99
Hauck, John, Brewing Co. 26
Hauck's beer 18
Hauser, John 70
Hayes, Rutherford B. 21
Hayna, Germany 58
Hebrew Union College 32
Hecker
    Friedrich 53
    Friedrich, statue of 79
Heckewelder, Johann 5
Heidelberg, Germany 3, 6, 48
Hemann, Joseph Anton 70
Henni, Johann Martin 11
Hermann, August 71
Hermannsschlacht/Battle of Hermann
    first major nativist riot 12
Hessian Benevolent Society 27
Hessischer Unterstuetzungsverein 27
Heuck, Hubert 21
Heuck's Opera House 21, 22
Hexamer, Dr. Charles 28
High German 12
Historical Collections of Ohio (Howe) 1

Hofbräuhaus Newport 41, 121
Holtgrewe, Henry 71
Holy Cross Parish 17
Holy Cross–Immaculata Church 17
Home for Aged Men 24
Honorary German Consul 40
Howe, Henry 7
Hudepohl, Ludwig 72
Huebener, Dr. Wilhelm 35, 72
Huenefeld Company 43, 72
Huenefeld, Ernst H. 43, 72, 73
Humboldt Street 61

I

I am the Resurrection and the Life 88, 97
ice cream
    Graeter's 129
Ich bin die Auferstehung und das Leben 88, 97
Immaculata 16, 76
immigration 8
Indiana 51
Institute of Catholic Art (Covington Altar Build Stock Co.) 18
International Folk Festival 108
International Program 115
internment of German-Americans 34
Iron Skillet 121

J

Jack Frost Accordion Band 119
Jahn
    Friedrich, 52
    Friedrich, Memorial Monument 52
Jergens
    Andrew 22, 78
    Andrew and Co. 22, 78
John A. Roebling Suspension Bridge 94
John Hauck Brewing Co. 26
Joseph-Beth Booksellers 133
journeyman's society 109
Jungle Jim's International Market 124, 129

K

Kahn, Elias 72
Kappelhoff
    Doris 67
    Wilhelm 67
Karkadoiulias 89
Kautz, August 72
Keim's Family Market 125
Kemper, Rev. James 72
Kent, Auguste 39
Kenton County Public Library 102, 106
King's Court 109
Kirchweih 107
Kitt family 58
Klaber, Franz 118

Klauprecht, Emil 12, 13, 15, 16, 72
Know-Nothings 13, 15, 16, 23, 106
Koehnken, A. and Grimm 52, 93
Kolping Band 109
Kolping Center 109
Kolping Grove 36, 37
Kolping Park 109
Kolping Saengerchor 52, 109
Kolping Society 31, 51, 109
Kolping Society Building 84
Kolping Society Groups
  Gold Club 109
  King's Court 109
  Kolping Band 109
  Kolping Saengerchor 109
  Kolping Sports Club 109
  Pigeon Club 109
  Schuetzen Club 109
  Senior Citizens 109
  Teen Club 109
  Tuesday Workers 109
  Young Adults 109
Kolping Sports Club 109
Kolping, Father Adolph 109
Korfingthan/Kurfingthan (Covington) family 7
Kraehling, Wilhelm 108
Kraemer Art Company 78
Kreimer's Bier Haus 121
Kreling, August von 56
Krienhagen 92
Kroger, Bernard 72
Kroschke, Hans 42
Kuehr
  Father Ferdinand 13, 97
  Monument 97
Kunwald, Ernst 72
Kunzel, Erich 41, 73

L

Ladbergen, Germany 43, 72
Lamprecht, Wilhelm 73
landscape gardening 77
Langen Meats 124
Langsam
  Julia 56, 95
  Walter 95
  Walter C. 36
Last Strike for Liberty, A Semi-Political Satire on the Revolutionary Demands of the Liberal Foreign Element, the (Robertson) 22
Lee, Robert E. 54
Lenhardt's Restaurant 62, 122
Leopoldine Mission Society of Vienna 52, 92
LeSourdsville Lake 108

Lessing Yearbook 40
Liberty Home 110
Liberty Home German Society 110
Liberty Home Society 110
Lincoln National Bank 61
Lincoln, Abraham 17, 18, 54
Lindbergh, Charles 65
Linden Noll Gift Haus 120
Lippert, Leon 74
literary society 5
Little Miami Publishing Co. 133
Loewenheim, Francis 32
Longworth, Nicholas 6, 100
Louisville 51
Louisville Platform 15
Low German 12
Lower Garden 18
Ludwig, Crown Prince of Bavaria 64
Luken, Tom 74
Lunken Airport 42, 65
Lunken, Edmund 42, 65
Lunkenheimer
  Company 42, 64
  Edmund 42, 65
  Eshelby 65
  Frederick 42, 64
  valves 64

M

M. Werk & Co. 9
Maifest 108
MainStrasse German Village 37, 63, 68, 89
Mann, Thomas 35
Map of Germany, Ohio 49
Markbreit family 24
markets
  Avril & Bleh Meat Market 123
  Findlay Market 124
  German Cuisine 124
  Hamman's Butcher Shop, Deli & Catering 124
  Hatting's Supermarket 125
  Jungle Jim's International Market 124
  Keim's Family Market 125
  Langen Meats 124
  Stehlin's Meat Market 124
  Wassler's Meat Market 125
Marlenheim in Alsace 9
Marshall Plan 39
Maurer, Helmut 108
Mause, Fred 108
Max Kade German Cultural Center 40
May Festival 13, 20, 29, 32, 51, 57, 58
Mayer and Co. 96
Mayer Royal Art Institute 93
mayor of Cincinnati
  Baum, Martin 5

Fleischmann, Julius 68
Springer, Jerry 76
Tafel, Gustaf 77
Ziegler, David 78
McCook, Robert L., statue of 79
Mecklenburg Biergarten 22
Mecklenburg Gardens 32, 61, 122
Mecklenburg, Louis 22
Meier, John M. 74
Meier's Wine Cellars, Inc. 129
Meier's Winery 74
Mein Tagebuch, Graded Readings for Beginners in German (Zeydel) 34
Melodies of German & Austria Program 115
Memorial Hall 19, 48
Meredith Street 61
Mexican War, formation of voluntary German units 13
Miami Exporting Company 4
Miami-Erie Canal 8
Mid-Morning with Wolf 116
militia companies 15
Miller, Ferdinand von 56
Minnesota, New Ulm 105
Minster, Ohio 62
Moeller High School 74
Moeller, Henry 27, 74
Moerlein Brewing Company 26, 59
Moerlein family 24
Moerlein, Christian 59, 62, 74, 81, 82
Moor, August 74
Moselle, explosion of 12
Mother of God Church 13, 52, 92
Mother of God Church Cemetery 88, 97
Mount Adams, Ohio 16, 76
Mount Storm Park 77
Muehlaeser family 24
Mueller-Fabricius, Victor 111
Muenster, Germany 127
Muer, Ferdinand 92
Munde
    Kypke 23
    Sophie 23
Munich, Germany 20, 39, 41, 52, 57, 92, 93, 96
Music Hall 20, 21, 29, 35, 41, 52, 74, 77, 80
Mutter Gottes Kirche 97

N

Napoleon I, French Emperor 53
Nast
    Methodistische Kirche 85
    Trinity Methodist Church 85
    Wilhelm 74, 85
National German-American Alliance 27, 104

National German-American Day, first celebration of 37, 38
National Register of Historic Places 56, 70
National Saengerfest 26, 36
National Song Festival 36
National Turnfest 28
Natur und Heimath (von Wahlde) 22
Neumann Way 74
Neumann, Gerhard 74
New Alsace, Indiana 62
New Orleans, Louisiana 47
    port city of 4
New Ulm, Minn. 14, 105
Newport, Ky. 19, 41
Nick Gulacsy (band) 116
Ninth Ohio Regiment 18, 19, 20, 54, 55, 77, 78, 80, 105
Nippert Stadium, building of 31
Nippert, A. K. 74, 104
North American Saengerbund 26, 32, 36
North American Turner Association/Turnerbund 105
North German Church 12
Northern Bank of Kentucky 96
Northern Cincinnati Convention & Visitors Bureau 113
Northern Kentucky Convention & Visitors Bureau 89, 114
Notre Dame 96
Nuernberg, Germany 32

O

Ohio Bicentennial Commission 41
Ohio Book Store 133
Ohio Chronik, Die 8
Ohio Daughters of the American Revolution 48
Ohio German-American Alliance 27
Ohio Historical Bicentennial Marker 43
Ohio Historical Society 40
    marker 30
Ohio River 12, 41
Ohio Valley, German Catholic churches of the 18
Ohlinger's 110
Oktoberfest 64, 107
    Cincinnati's original 108
    Minster, Ohio 62
    Munich, Germany 64
Old St. Mary's Church 52, 70, 83, 119
Oldenburg, Germany 62
Oldenburg, Indiana 62
oldest
    German-American society in Cincinnati 105
    Turner Society in America 105
One Hundredth Annual German Day 40

Opening Day 82
Order of Merit 36
Osnabrueck, Germany 12, 39, 57
OTR Ale Haus 44
Ott, Franziska C. 40
Otto von Bismarck, tree planted in honor of
24
Over-the-Rhine 75, 79
8, 9, 13, 18, 19, 20, 31, 48, 50, 52, 53, 57,
74, 79
Day 108
Over-the-Rhine Showcase 42, 108, 115

P

Pacific Garden 18
Palatinate 10
Party Source 130
Pastorius Day 103
Pastorius, Franz Daniel 103
*Peace or Appeasement? Hitler, Chamber-
lain, and the Munich Crisis* (Loewen-
heim) 32
Peaslee, John B. 24
Pennsylvania German
pietists 48
soldiers 3
Pennsylvania Germans 5
Pershing/Bremen St. 92
Pete Wagner Band 118
Pfaender, Wilhelm 105
Philadelphia, Penn. 47
port city of 4
Philippus Kirche 82
Philippus United Church of Christ 82
Pieper, Charlotte 74
Pigeon Club 109
Pionier-Verein (German Pioneer Society)
103
Polka Dots (band) 119
Poole, Marge 114
Pope Leo XIII 93
Postl, Karl Anton (aka Sealsfield, Charles) 8
Potsdam Military Academy 54
Prince of Peace Lutheran Church 84
Probasco estate 55
Probasco, Henry 56
Probst, Heinz 42
Prochnow
Fritz 108
LaNelle 108
Prohibition 31, 32, 59, 61, 94, 106
Pros't Band 118
Protestant, Der 11
Prussian Army 55
Public Library of Cincinnati & Hamilton
County 36, 102
Purcell, John 16

Q

Queen City Club 29

R

radio programs, German-American 42
Rahn, A. J., Greenhouses 130
Rattermann, Heinrich A. 21, 57, 75, 83, 103
Rattermann-Strasse, H. A. 39
Reagan, Ronald 38, 64
proclamation for German-American Day
37
Reemelin, Charles 75
Reese, Rev. Dr. Friedrich 76
Reform Judaism 78
Refugee Scholars Project 32
Regina Bakery 129
Rehfuss, Ludwig 10
Reichrath Park 51
Reiner, Fritz 76
Remus, George 31
Repeal (of Prohibition) 59
Rese, Dr. Friedrich 7
restaurants and cafes
120
Black Forest Restaurant 120
Brau Haus 121
Brotzeit Deli 120
German Cuisine 121
Germantowne Pizza Haus 121
Hofbräuhaus Newport 121
Iron Skillet 121
Kreimer's Bier Haus 121
Lenhardt's Restaurant 122
Mecklenburg Gardens 122
Ron's Roost 122
Sherman House 122
Steinkeller 122
Strasse Haus 122
Wertheim's Restaurant 123
Wiener Haus 123
Rice University 32
Riedlin, William 94
Robertson, John 22, 23
Roebling
Johann August 19, 95
John A. 95
John Augustus 45
monument 95
Suspension Bridge 19, 45, 55, 94, 95
Roedter, Heinrich 10, 13, 76
Ron's Roost 122
Royal Academy of Fine Arts 57, 96
Royal Military Academy 55
Rudolf, Max 76
Ruehlmann, Eugene 76

S

Saengerfest 36, 51
Saengerfest-Halle 80
Saenger-Halle 20
Saint Johannes-Gemeinde 12
Saint Marien Kirche 83
Saint Xavier College 7
Salem Church of Christ 82
Salem German Evangelical Reformed
    Church 82
Sawyer Point 41
Saxe-Hildburghausen 64
Saxony Imports 120
Scarlet Oaks (retirement home) 43
Schade, Richard Erich 40
Schickling's 18
Schiller
    celebration 16, 29
    Friedrich 16
Schlaraffia 111
Schlaraffia Cincinnatia 111
Schlaraffia Society 111
Schmidlapp family 24
Schmidt
    Charles G. 32, 76
    Charles G. (photo) 33
Schmidt, Peggy 33
Schmitt, Johann 17, 52, 76, 92
schnecken 125
Schneider, Herman 76
Schott, Marge 76
Schottelkotte, Al 76
Schroeder
    Frederick 93
    Henry 93
Schuetzen
    Club 109
    Company 105
Schuetzenfest 19
Schuler's 18
Schumann Street 61
Schumann's 18
Schumann-Heink, Ernestine 32
Schurz, Carl 21
Schwaab, John 27, 104
Schwab, Ernst 108
Sealsfield, Charles (aka Postl, Karl Anton) 8
Seasongood/Suessengut, Jacob 76
Second World War 104
Senior Citizens 109
Servatii's Bakery 62
Sharon Woods Village 72
Sherman House 122
Shinkle, Amos 95
Shinkle's Row 95
Sidewalk King (Weishaupt, Christian) 31

Significant Books 133
Sinton, David 100
Sioux Uprising of 1862 (Dakota Conflict)
    14
Sixth District School 80
soap king 78
Society for German-American Studies 37
Society for the Acclimatization of Birds 56
Society for the Needy Children of Central
    Europe 31
society for the promotion of agriculture 5
Spirit of St. Louis. 65
Spring Grove Cemetery 55, 74, 77
Spring Grove Cemetery and Aboretum 131
Springer
    Jerry 76
    Reuben 21, 77
St. Augustine's Church 25
St. Clair, Arthur 4
St. Francis Seminary 109
St. Johannes-Gemeinde 7
St. John's Protestant Church 79, 84
St. John's Unitarian Church 7
St. Marien Kirche 83
St. Paul Church 83
St. Paul's German Evangelical Church 84
Staebler, Johannes 6
Stallo, John B. 18, 77
steam fire engines 67
Steger, Joseph 77
Stegner, Clarence 82
Stegner's Meat store 82
Stehlin's Meat Market 124
Stein, Albert von 77
Steinkeller 122
Stern, Guy 77
Steuben
    Hall 104
    House 111
Store to Explore 132
Strasse Haus 122
Strauch, Adolph 55, 77
Strauss Ball 107
street name changes 61
Stucken, Frank van der 77
Stuttgarter Hochschule für Musik 57, 67
Sunday blue laws 23
Supreme Court decision 31
Suspension Bridge 19
Swabians 7

T

Tafel
    family 24
    Gustaf 77
Taft
    family 100

Mrs. 29
Museum of Art 5, 47, 67, 100
William H. 29
Taft Road 61
Tappert
    Rev. Henry 93
    Rev. William 93
Teen Club 109
Tell City, Ind. 14
Teutopolis, Ill. 14
Teutscher Calender auf 1808 6
Therese, Princess of Saxe-Hildburghausen
    64
Thien, Wenceslaus 92
Third German Protestant Memorial Church
    12
Third Reich, refugees of the 32
Thirty-second Indiana German Regiment
    20, 55, 78
Thomas, Theodore 29, 42, 57
Toebben, Matth. 95
Tolzmann, Don Heinrich 37, 38
Trinity Church 84
Tri-State German-American School 108
    Society 36
Truppach, Bavaria, Germany 59
Tuesday Workers 109
Turner
    Fest 105
    Hall 13, 21, 93, 104, 105
    Movement 53
    School 105
    Society 52, 80
Turnerbund 105
Turnerism 34
Turners 18
Turnverein 52
Twachtman, John Henry 77
Twenty-eighth Ohio Regiment 74
Twenty-fifth National Turnfest 24
Twenty-third Corps of the Union Army 72
Tyler Davidson Fountain 56
    dedication of 20

U

U.S. Army of the Potomac 78
Ullrich, Charles F. 78
Unification of Germany
    celebration of 40
Union Army 53, 54
Union Terminal 100
Union, the 18
United Church of Christ 93
United States Minister to Italy 77
Universal German Assistance Club 110
University of Cincinnati 26, 31, 32, 36, 37,
    40

Blegen Library 102
College Conservatory of Music 67
    cooperative education 76
    German Department 77
    German Exile Literature 77
    German-American Studies 77
    German-Americana Collection 68, 81
    Schmidt rooms 76

V

Van Buren, Martin 13
Vater Rhein (Rattermann) 58
Vereinigten Staaten, Die von Nordamerika
    (Sealsfield/Postl) 8
Vevay, Indiana 7
Vienna, Austria 53
Virginia Bakery 125
visitors' centers
    Cincinnati USA & Visitors Bureau 113
    Northern Cincinnati Convention & Visi-
        tors Bureau 113
    Northern Kentucky Convention & Visi-
        tors Bureau 114
Volksblatt 10, 13, 29
Volksfreund, Der 70
Volstead Act 31
von Bismarck, Otto 19
von Wahlde, Hermann 22
von Willich, August 17, 20

W

Wahlde, Hermann von 22
Wahrheits-Freund, Der 70
Walburg, Rev. A. H. 25
Waldenbooks 133
Waldschmidt
    Christian 48, 99
    House 48, 99
Waldschmidt, Christian 5
War for Independence 48
Wartburg, Tenn. 14
Washington Park 20, 53, 79, 80
Wassler's Meat Market 125
waterworks 77
Wegerer, Alfred von 34
Weishaupt, Christian 31
Weitzel, Gottfried 78
Werk
    Castle 78
    Castle Lane 78
    M. and Co. 78
    Michael 9, 78
    Road 78
Werk's Tag Soap 9
Wertheim, Sal 62
Wertheim's Restaurant 62, 123
West Fork Park 40, 51

Western Museum 5
Western Spy 3
Westlicher Merkur 10
Wiedemann, George, Brewing Co. 26
Wielert
    family 24
    Henry 18
Wielert's (beer hall) 18
Wielert's Beer Hall 18
Wiener Haus 123
Wilhelm II, King of Prussia 35, 72
Wilhelm Tell 29
Willich, August von 17, 20, 54, 78
Windholtz, Christy 62
Windhorst, Kansas 14
Windisch
    beer 59
    Conrad 59
Windisch-Muehlhauser Brewing Co. 26
Wise, Isaac Meyer 78

Wittke, Carl 14
Wolff Printing Co., 96
Women's Auxiliary of Covington Turners
    106
Wooden Shoe Hollow 130
Wooden Shoe Hollow (Pieper) 74
Woodland Cemetery 3
Woodrow Street 61
Works Progress Administration (WPA) 31
World Since 1914, The (Langsam) 36
World War I 25, 30, 32, 36, 61
World War II 25, 34
Wurlitzer, Howard 31

Y

Young Adults 109

Z

Zeydel, Edwin H. 34, 78
Ziegler, David 3, 6, 48, 78

About the Author

DON HEINRICH TOLZMANN is the Curator of the German-Americana Collection and Director of the German-American Studies Program at the University of Cincinnati. He is the author and editor of numerous works relating to German-American history and culture, including several for the Cincinnati and Northern Kentucky area.

Dr. Tolzmann is shown standing next to the Cincinnati monument that honors Friedrich Hecker, a leader of the 1848 Revolution in Germany. In Cincinnati, Hecker and other Forty-eighters established the first Turner Society in America.

·